SKYROCKET YOUR BRAND

30 Days to Write, Publish & Market Your Book

GAIL THACKRAY

Layout and design and cover art by Teagarden Designs

Printed in the United States of America

Thackray, Gail

Skyrocket your Brand:
30 Days to Write, Publish & Market Your Book

Published by
Indian Springs Publishing
451 N Cannon Drive,
Beverly Hills
CA 90210

www.indianspringspublishing.com

LAUNCH YOUR BRAND AND 100X YOUR INCOME

What a Book Can Do for You

Do you have a powerful mission that you want to share? Do you have a story that you are dying to tell? Would you like to be a top life coach or a sought-after speaker? Do you have a business or a product and would you like to see your sales go through the roof?

Writing a non-fiction book can raise your profile exponentially. It solidifies your personal brand and creates a backstory and personal identity to any business or product, making you an influencer. It is quite extraordinary how writing a book can increase your profile dramatically.

Whether you are promoting a company, product or you as a personal brand, a book is an extremely valuable tool you can't afford to be without. If a person reads your book and is impressed with what they learn, they will be seeking you out, hoping to meet you and can't wait to attend your workshops or purchase your products.

Even if you are already a speaker, a coach or have an existing business, publishing a book takes you from the place of being somebody knowledgeable, to being an expert. It is very easy for anyone to publish a book these days, yet the public still views a "published author" as an expert. It instantly places you on a pedestal, where people hang on your every word. There is nothing better than publishing a book to give you instant credibility, skyrocket your brand, and get you a stream of customers!

❖

Publishing a book can launch your career as a coach or speaker and can literally 100x your income!

❖

What does this mean in terms of dollars? This can completely launch your business and brand to instant profitable success. This can create your career as a speaker, a coach, or a guru in your chosen field. For those already speaking, coaching or promoting a business, this can literally 100x your income!

Finding Your Passion

I am going to presume you already know what you would like to write about. That you are already sharing your story on some level, or have a business or product with a back-story, or you are well versed in a subject that you would like to share. You are just having difficulty getting started or in the mechanics of actually getting your book on paper.

If this is not the case, and you are not sure what you want to write about, then you need to dig deep. Think about what you know the most about, or what you could easily teach or share and what you are excited about. What experiences have you had, especially difficult experiences that you can share about that will help people or motivate people or give them hope?

You may feel that your story is not that dramatic. That is ok. Be genuine and authentic. Even if your story is about being a mom and dealing with teenagers or children, or as a wife, or as a dog sitter and your events don't seem that relevant, if you tell your story from an authentic place people will relate and that is of great interest to your audience.

If you are sharing knowledge you may feel that you are not yet qualified enough. Even if there are others in your field that you feel are more credible or better at the subject than you, it doesn't matter. You have a voice and people want to hear it. Don't ever wait, thinking that you have to become more knowledgeable or that you are not at the place of being an expert yet because someone else is more qualified than you. People relate to people more than to someone's expertise. If you do a good job of sharing your experience and people relate to you they will follow you just as much as someone who had more experience than you.

If you have a product that you sell, what is it that makes this so special? People relate to people and their stories, not to products. The reason you decided to launch your business, why you developed your product and why you are passionate about it, is the thing that customers want to know. People buy into you, your story, your experience, your passion and how that relates to their life. And your book is where you can share your story.

❖

What do you know that you can share and what are you passionate about?

❖

Your book is going to make you an expert in this field and open up doors to speak about it, or create a product you can represent, so be sure this is what you are really passionate about. You must be passionate about the subject of your book. It is hard enough to keep yourself on track, so you need that drive. When you love the subject you are writing about, writing this book will be fun.

Why Non-Fiction
"How to" books and Journal True-life Experience books

The primary aim of this book is to raise your brand awareness. It's not really about writing an amazing book or winning any literary awards. The goal is all about you. The book is a stepping-stone that has to be positioned perfectly to set your career on fire.

We are going to concentrate on "how to" books. Meaning those where you impart knowledge and are sharing and teaching what you know. And we are also going to talk about non-fictional "journey" or true-life story books, where you are taking the reader on an adventure or experience that you have had. A journey book, may be written in a time-line format or a collection of experiences that you've had, ultimately sharing knowledge or inspiration with the reader.

> ❖
>
> If you are looking to write the next best novel, this book is not for you.
>
> ❖

If you are looking to write the next best novel, this book is not for you. You will find structure and tips here that will make writing any kind of book faster and easier, but I am really concentrating on books that will catapult your career outside of your book.

Who Am I?

If I can write a book, anyone can!

I don't profess to be some incredible author. On the contrary, I still find it difficult to consider myself a "writer," even though I've published 15 "best sellers." And that's the point! If I can do this, anyone can. I can't spell. I was a science major in school, not creative at all, and English was definitely not my forte. I would never have guessed I would ever write a book. So how did I get into this? Well, I sort of fell into a career in meta-physics. I previously had a successful tech company and went on a tangent exploration of spiritual subjects on my own search for spiritual growth. I was asked to share what I knew and speak about natural healing, and pretty soon I was giving workshops and lectures. And this was all before I wrote any books.

At the end of a lecture, people would come up and tell me how much they loved the talk and thank me and then that was it, nothing to sell, nothing to offer them. When I finally published a book, I did a lecture, and as I finished my talk, instead of just coming up to say "hi," I had a line of people waiting to buy my book and get my autograph! It was amazing, and what was even more amazing was they kept my book, read my book, and contacted me because of the book. Suddenly I had emails, I had customers, I had a "following." I realized that I was an expert in their mind. And when I released my second book, those same people couldn't wait to buy my next book. I realized in that moment, how publishing a book was a game changer for me.

But was I an expert? There were certainly people who knew a lot more about the subjects I wrote about than I did. In fact, this whole meta-physical thing started out for me as a personal exploration. I was interested in the subject and went searching out of my own curiosity and my own soul seeking. I realized, what I learned along the way was very interesting to others. And it wasn't just about the final outcome and what I learned, but people wanted to know about the journey, the experience, and see what it was like to learn alongside me. If I had waited until I thought I was really knowledgeable about something, I would never have written a book. I'd still be waiting for me to get better than those I see as more knowledgeable than me.

After people read the book, many said they found it easy to relate to me because they said I write like I talk. That my personality comes through and people loved that. It was actually the fact that my books were down to earth, often admitting to my own insecurities and inadequacies that people loved. They didn't want to be lectured at. They didn't want to feel that I was untouchable, they wanted to relate.

Are my books literary works to be proud of? No! Do they have the odd grammatical error or sentences that could have been worded better? Sure! But people love them, and that's the point. If you are looking for literary perfection, I am not the best coach for you. People can spend years making their book perfect. For me, good is good enough. The point for me is to get the word out in books that people love and to get it out fast. For me it is not about winning a Pulitzer prize it's about getting your voice to the world. It is about using your book to share your voice and give you the platform.

I have since written several "how to" type non-fiction books on metaphysical subjects: new age, wellness, natural healing and manifesting. I've also written several, what I call journey books, which are time-line stories of adventures I have experienced. Yes, these are all in the new age realm but what I actually learned about writing itself, the process, and publishing, applies to any genre. And my last book was an expose comedy in the vein of "Wolf of Wall Street" which was a very different genre!

❖

I fell into every writer's trap. I wish I had this book when I started writing, it would have saved me months!

❖

Oh, how I wished I could have had a plan or a manual, before I began. I learned through trial and error. I fell in all the writer pit falls. I made all the mistakes. It took me months longer than it should have, because I was simply working backwards. How I wish I had had a road map. So here it is, and this is why I wrote this book!

How to Use This Book

I have first given you an overview of some of the principles you are going to need to know before you put pen to paper. Then I describe the system that will save you a ton of time and show you how to avoid all the energy draining, time consuming traps, that almost all writers fall into. I will walk you through a specific plan of action and the details of the exact steps you need to take.

I know you probably want to jump right in to the 30 Day plan but I recommend that you at least browse through this first part of the book.

After you have completed the 30 days, I share secrets to uploading your book that will guarantee a Best Seller launch and the real scoop on marketing your book for instant success.

- Secrets you need to know before you put pen to paper
- 30 Day Plan of Action, guaranteed to get your book done
- The real scoop on marketing to maximize your success

Making the Big Bucks

Do books make money? A lot of people say you don't make much money, is that true?

There are writers who make a good living out of just writing non-fiction books. These are often prolific non-fiction writers, who knock out multiple books, like a book every few weeks and have a definite system in their marketing. These type of system-writers are making money from their series of books. Some books might make just a little money, and some may bring in bigger profits, collectively, hopefully, reaping a lucrative income. These serial non-fiction writers are counting on making money from the book sales themselves. Often they are not even familiar with a subject but will rather study it for the purpose of writing a series of books and then move on to another area to write about. Sometimes they will use different fictitious names for each series. These writers don't care about brand awareness, they simply care about the money coming off each book.

But then you hear that other people wrote a great book and after publishing it, it just sat there and did nothing. This is true. There are certain key elements you absolutely need in your book to make it sell and there are essential considerations you need in navigating distribution and marketing. Without these key ingredients, very few books make any sales.

So yes, if you know what you are doing, you can make money from the sale of books, good money, and I will explain the hidden secrets to make the most profits. However, this is not our end game. This is not you. I believe you care about the branding and the recognition from your book. Yes, I will show you how to make money on your book sales, but there is something of far more importance. The money you stand to gain on the back end from the increased awareness about you and your story, is far more valuable.

I am going to presume that most of you reading this are interested in widening your audience and creating more money through speaking gigs and selling services and products, rather than the profits from the book itself. If not, you should be! But if you are interested in simply making money through your books you can use the steps I am sharing here and that will work well for you. You may even use these steps to speed up your book production from 30 days to a book a week. However, we are going to concentrate on not only speed, but very high quality, so I am suggesting 30 days to complete this. And your book is going to absolutely brand you.

Your book is your calling card. If your customers received your brochure, they are going to view that as a sales pitch. But if you gave them a book, they would view it as a gift that has content, something of value. And yet its real value for you is to share your message, your personality, and your backstory, with your customers, which is ultimately much more valuable. There is nothing more important to a business than a book. There is

❖

The money you stand to gain on the back end from the increased awareness about you and your story is the real gold.

❖

nothing that will raise your brand and profile more than having your story as a book. Getting your book in the hands of your customers, even if you need to give it away, is going to bring back your profits a hundred-fold.

And you probably won't stop at one book and shouldn't. Once you have published one book you can expand to write about other areas of your knowledge or go vertical with a future book to take your customers more in-depth. But there is no faster way to instant credibility, than becoming a published author.

I am going to show you the secrets to making your book sell, but not because you care about the profits from the book, you care about your name, your brand and your market share where the profits are a hundred times greater.

IS THE MARKET BEGGING FOR MY BOOK?

Publishing Deals in the Toilet

This book is going to concentrate on the new world of self-publishing, distribution, and marketing. Over the last few years publishing has changed tremendously. In the old days you would have been advised to prepare a chapter sample, a structure outline and introduction blurb. Then you would probably seek out lists of agents or go direct to publishers. You'd expect to receive a ten-thousand-dollar advance to write the book, and then sit back and collect royalties. Don't expect that anymore.

To get to the top publishers like Simon and Schuster or Harper Collins, you would need an absolutely amazing story. So, unless you have a story like you slept with the President, it will be a hard road to go. Even with a fantastic story they will ask you "What marketing do you have?" In other words, how many Instagram followers do you have, how many Facebook followers do you have, and how many Twitter followers do you have? And if you don't have a million of those, you can forget it. Of course, if you are booked on some major TV show they might be interested.

Yes, there are some smaller publishers, and in some cases they may be appropriate for your niche, but the deals are just not as good as they used to be. They will expect you to do a large amount of the publicity on your own dime, but if you are good at that, then you might not need them. It's a catch 22.

If you are an established speaker or you need a large amount of books to gift to your clients or to sell at your events, the dollars may not make sense. For example, if you go through a book publisher, you are likely to receive around $1 royalty per book sale. On the other hand, you may wish to have a certain number of books for yourself to give or sell to your customers. Now that you are exclusive with a publisher, you have to buy your own books at wholesale cost from the publisher. For example, if your book sells for $14.95 and the printing costs are $3 and you need 10,000 books a year to sell to your people or give away, your cost would normally be just the printing $30,000. And you may need this amount of books every year. Now if you have a publishing deal in place, you probably have to buy your own books through them, and you are not allowed to go direct to the printer. If the book sells retail for $14.95, you probably have to pay $7.00 for each of your own books you want to buy (even though the printing is only $3). To buy the same amount of books would cost you around $70,000, an increase of $40,000. That means your publisher would have to sell 40,000 books, giving you $40,000 before you break even on your own books that you are selling. I am not telling you not to go through a publisher, but you want to weigh up exactly what your intention is with your book. Generally if you are very active in selling your book, and you plan to order a lot of units for yourself, (which I hope you will when you have finished my book), then you may be better off self-publishing.

❖

How much work are you willing to do yourself? That is the question.

❖

Also, some publishers may be banking on you becoming a speaker from your books and may actually get a percentage of that revenue. That's great if they are also helping you with marketing. Again, make sure you understand any deal you get into. When I first started and I didn't yet have a book, I had some interest from a large TV company to do a series. My attorney pointed out to me that it was a good idea to have a book published and a track record of speaking, otherwise it is standard that the TV show would be entitled to a large portion of your book revenues and speaking monies.

Competition, Demand and Doing Your Own Thing

There are programs such as publisherrocket.com that will help you decipher how much interest there is in your subject and how many books are already on the market. You can type in your subject matter and it will pull up similar books on kindle and how many of each book have been sold. However, if your primary goal is to increase your profile, I don't think you need to consider this. You will write what you are passionate about and what you are knowledgeable about and share your story. Remember your book is really your calling card for people to get to know you.

Publisherrocket.com is a great program to get for many other features though. It is a one-time charge about $95 and is really useful for finding key words or terms searched specifically on Amazon and most important features that will put your book in the right position to become an instant "Amazon Best Seller."

If your book appeals to a very finite niche group, that is fine, you may have a smaller audience, but those interested in your niche are more likely to be interested in your book and you. If your Market is large such as you are a life coach or a fitness Guru, then you should try to find a hook or an angle within your market. And this goes for you as a speaker or coach, just as you need a hook in your book, you need a hook in your services. Do you have an incredible story of how you overcame obstacles or do you have a track record of how you helped others, or do you have a special technique which is going to make someone achieve their goals faster and easily.

As human beings we are all about, how can we get short cuts, do something better or more easily or for less money or for less work? How can we overcome obstacles, and perhaps we can learn from others who have gone through something similar to me? So, what makes you and your book, and your story stand out? What are you offering people? Does your book make people accomplish something, make money, lose weight, be smarter, be more loveable, and does your book help them to do this faster, easily and for less money?

❖

Your book
is your
calling card.

Does your book
make people
accomplish
something,
make money,
lose weight,
be smarter, be
more loveable?
Faster, easier
and for
less money?

❖

MY SECRET SYSTEM TO WRITING YOUR WILDLY SUCCESSFUL BOOK, QUICKLY & EASILY

Structure, Structure, Structure

I am going to show you how to write your book quickly and easily, from initial concept, to getting it on paper. Everything you need from start to finish, avoiding all the usual pit falls that leave your book hanging for months, even years. I am going to show you how to include the key elements that will make your book a best seller. You will learn structure, how to motivate yourself and spark your creativity, plus, tricks to make your content a page turner. I am going to teach you the secrets to successful publishing and marketing and how to include key elements you must have before you put pen to paper. We're going to concentrate on non-fiction "how to" type books, and non-fiction journal or true-life experience books, but many tips you will learn here can be applied to all types of books.

Secrets You will Learn:

- The secret system that will save you hours
- How to find your highly creative zone
- Discover your true writing personality
- Speed writing: fast, flowing, creative
- How to combat writer's block
- Develop your structure, cut out months of struggle
- Make your book a page turner
- Create a book that gets you instant credibility
- How to design a cover that stands out and sells
- Secret tips to maximize profits
- Avoid losing money in publishing traps
- Time saving tips, programs & latest author tech help
- Resources you can't afford not to have
- Marketing secrets no one else will share
- Easy trick to becoming an instant Best Seller

SECRETS YOU NEED TO KNOW BEFORE YOU START

Research, Steal and Plagiarize

Not really! When you have decided what you are going to write about, it is time to do some research. Going through Amazon, you can see what books have already been published in your genre. You might want to purchase some of them and see what you personally like about them, or don't like about them. Also check out the reviews and see if others have the same thoughts as you. Concentrate on the 3 and 4 star reviews as they will give an indication of what the readers want, that this book lacks. 5 star reviews are glowing fans, and 1 and 2 star reviews are just miserable human-beings who have no life.

You may also find some ideas that you want to steal. Just kidding. You don't want to copy anyone else's work, but you might find some interesting gems that you hadn't thought to include. Make notes on a

❖

Keep a note pad handy as you research books by others.

❖

27

separate pad, as you are reading so you don't forget. Jot down notes as you come across concepts that you want to remember to put in your book. You might find some useful tips on things you want to make sure you include. Also pay attention to the layout and format that you found most appealing. Look at the layout; what stands out to you? What draws you in? What makes you want to keep reading? Also check out the book titles, chapter titles, and cover art that you like.

Should I Hold Back Some of My Secret Sauce?

People sometimes wonder if you give away all your secrets in the book, then why would people want to hire you as say a coach, or go to your workshops, if this information is already available in your book. Even if the nuggets of your knowledge are already in the book, if the person is engaged in your content, they want to have that one-on-one connection with you even more. I believe you should give them as much content and useful information as you possibly can and do not hold back. The more someone gets out of your book, the more excited they are going to be to learn more from you and to find out more about you. The truth is even if you give them everything, they are still not going to do it all on their own anyway, they need you. And you may think

> ❖
> Fill your book with as much knowledge as you can, and blow their mind.
>
> ❖

that blowing all your information on one book, you will not be able to write a second book. Believe me, you will find more information to write about in the future.

Ghostwriter or Ghastly Writer

You don't have to be a trained writer to write a book, especially a non-fiction book. Almost anyone can write a book these days. The problems usually arise with getting started because it can be over-facing. The system I have outlined here will make it so much easier for you. Yes, you can hire a ghost writer to write for you. They are going to cost you anywhere from $500 to $3,000 and up, but you get what you pay for and you need to pay

❖

Consider a
Copy Editor
instead

❖

the top to get anyone decent otherwise it is going to be ghastly writing. However, I really think that you should have the first crack at it. You know your material better than anyone and even if you get a ghost writer you will spend time tweaking it. If you write it yourself, you can always hire a copy editor, which is where they will make the most difference. But with the tips I'm going to show you, you'll see how easy it is to write it completely yourself. You can even voice record some of it. You are the closest to your material. This is your personality, and your personality needs to come out in the right way.

Incorporating Public Domain Titles

A US copyright lasts for 95 years. Therefore, any books first published prior to 95 years ago, become public domain. As of January 1st 2021, all books published in 1925 and earlier will become public domain. This means that you can legally take a book from that time and republish it. You can also create your own combination of a public domain book and your own writing. You could make money just republishing these books, though as you will see there are many other people who have already republished almost every book. Each January 1st, a new group of books will become public domain and you will see a bunch of publishers re-publishing those books, as well as creating movies and TV shows from them. Still you may find a

❖

TIP–You may find pdfs of these books on the web. Someone has at one time transcribed these into the pdf. If you are going to use one of these pdfs you will find there are often many errors that you will need to correct by comparing it to the original book or one published by a respected publisher. Also, be careful as there may be additional text added in by another author that may not be in the public domain.

❖

creative way to incorporate a public domain book into your own books.

Hot Title

Your title is extremely important, but we are not going to address this today. We are going to do some research and I will show you how to find out the buzz words that sell and we'll go through how to use Google Trends and programs like publisherrocket.com but for now don't give it much thought, just give it a working title.

Size Does Matter

How many pages should you write? We are concentrating on "how to" type books or non-fictional books that present your story or message, perhaps in a journal type manner. A person looking for a self-help, how-to type book is interested in learning as much as they can, in as short a period as possible. Therefore, they want to know from the cover blurbs and forward, exactly what they will learn. They need to know what their final outcome is going to be. They want to know exactly what knowledge they will have and also an estimate of how much time this is going to cost them.

The reader wants to know that they will be getting a large amount of knowledge, or knowledge that is not readily available. They also consider their time valuable and so they want to learn this as quickly as possible. If a book appears to the reader to be "too thick," meaning it has a lot of pages, the reader may think it is going to be too difficult and over-whelming or that it may have too much fluff. Summary books work great in this "how-to" genre, because people perceive they are still getting the knowledge they need, but without any time wasting. Your book should not look like it has too many pages. However too little pages and they may wonder if there is enough knowledge contained in your book. These days people value their time to read your book as much more valuable than the cost of the book itself.

Your "how to" book should be between 150 and 250 pages in the finished book. This equates to about double that on a Word Doc page, so between 75 and125 Word Doc pages. Text is on average 500 words per Word Doc page, so if you had just text on a page, that would work out at about 37,500 to 62,500 words total. However, in a "how to" book you are going to add illustrations and spread out the copy to make it visually appealing, so you will need a lot less text. I would aim to give your designer 50-100 pages of Word Doc text (25,000 to 50,000 word count) which will expand to fit more pages in the final layout.

Don't worry right now about the page count while you are writing, follow the steps I advise through the copyediting stage, and then do a word count. If you are under 25,000 words, you could expand some of your concepts, or see if there are additional items you want to include. Do not add fluff. You are better off spreading out your design a little more.

If you are doing a "how to" type book and you are at 70,000 words or more, I would start editing out any fluff and slashing sections, as this is going to be too long and too much for the average "how to" book. Of course, there are exceptions, where you are offering more ways to do something, more ideas etc. Where the reader might hope for more information. These are just guidelines for the average "how to" book where the reader learns something.

It is also important for a "how-to" book to layout the information in easily digestible chunks. Non-fiction readers love words to be arranged with lists and blocks and spaces and the use of bold and italics, so that important items are high-lighted and most important thoughts can be easily scanned and referenced. Big chunks of text are going to look too difficult to absorb. Spreading out the text will add to the number of pages in your book, so take this into account. I would do a full line of space for each new paragraph as opposed to an indention paragraph that you would use in a novel or in a journey book.

If you are writing a fictional novel this page number would not apply. In fact, it is quite the opposite, many people want a big thick book. When they are buying a novel, they are buying a book for hours of entertainment, the longer the better, as this equates to more hours of enjoyment.

❖

Non-Fiction "How to" Book

150 to 250 pages in the finished book

50 to 100 Word Doc pages

25,000 to 50,000 words with text spread out

Non-Fiction Journey Type Book

250 to 350 pages in the finished book

125 to 175 Word Doc pages

62,500 to 87,500 words

❖

In a non-fiction, journal type book, your layout will be somewhere in between. A journal book is a cross between a "how-to" book and a novel. You would not expect as much of an interesting layout as a "how-to" book, but some structure would be good. The more your book reads like a timeline novel that happens to be true, the more you need to keep your design simple and more pages will be acceptable. For a journey type book, aim for 250 to 350 pages in the finished book, which equates to 125 to175 Word Doc pages, and 62,500 to 87,500 words. If at the copyediting stage you have too little words, think about creatively expanding your sentences. Think about how you could go into more description, bringing more detail to each sentence. In a journey book, too many words is not too much of a problem. Just make sure all the events in your book are interesting and if not, you can cut out some sections.

Your Voice, Your Style

You are going to be more comfortable writing in the way you speak. This brings out your personality. Of course, it depends what subject you are writing about, but I think most of the time, bringing out your personality is a good thing.

If you are writing a "how to" book, generally you are going to write as if you were explaining to someone, or as if you were doing a talk to a group. That is, you are in teacher mode, but that doesn't mean you can't have personality. People don't just want to learn, that sounds too much like school.

But before you get into teacher mode, the reader first wants to know who you are, so here is where you capture their interest to learn from you specifically. If you have a track record and are famous for what you are teaching, then great, but if not you need to share your story so they feel validated that they bought your book and they are anxious to learn from you. Telling your story about why you got into something or your personal experience that changed your life, or how you discovered that secret sauce you are going to explain, captures their attention. In a "how to" book, this can be done as a story at the beginning of the book. In a journey type book, your entire book may be your story, your experience, your adventure with a message that comes out through the book that motivates them, entertains them, or moves them.

When you are telling your story at the beginning or writing a journal book you have the choice of writing it in the first person, or as if you were someone else telling your story in the third person. If it is about you, I believe it is much better to write it as yourself in the first person. "I couldn't believe what I saw and I...," as opposed to writing about you, "She couldn't believe what she saw and she..."

Now what tense should you write in? In the past? Or as if it is happening now in the present? This may take a bit of finesse. It is easier to write in the past as the event happened in the past, but I believe if you write in the present tense, as if you are there right now, it draws the reader in as if it is happening now. This may be a little more difficult. You would be writing, "and here I am, as I look around I see..." But you probably need to set the reader up to know this is what you are doing. But then you can also use flash backs to the past. For example, "this made me remember the time when ..."

In general, if it is a short story about how you did something that brought you to this realization, such as in an intro to a how-to book, I would tell it in the past. If your entire book is a journal, I would write it in the present. But play around with this by writing some samples and see what you feel is best.

❖

Let the reader hear your personality

❖

The most important thing is to try not to mix tenses unless done very deliberately, going back and forth between tenses with no explanation, gets confusing to the reader.

Making it a Page Turner

You may think if someone bought your book, they are for sure going to read it, right? Wrong. How many books have you bought that sit around for months before you read it? Remember it is not about just selling books, it is about the promotion it gives you. This only works if they read it. And once they start reading it, you need them to keep reading it! You want to create a page turner that they rave about. You need to be very aware to create every opportunity to make the reader read on.

You need:

- In a "how to book" Let them know up front what they will be learning so they can get excited and motivated to read it. You can do this at the beginning of the book with a list of what they will learn. In some books it might be appropriate to also add what they will learn at the beginning of each chapter as well.

- In a "how to book" keep the chapters short so they feel they have easily finished and digested that information. It makes them willing to attempt another chapter or lesson, so they will go on to the next chapter.

- Having your chapters as numbered steps or days, helps to get them to keep reading if this works with your format.

- Create catchy chapter titles. In a journey type book, the chapters should have intrigue and surprise and not be the titles you would expect. In a "how to" informational book, the chapter headers could be very interesting as well, or they could be very clear, so the reader knows exactly the information he is getting in that chapter.

- In a "how to" book you may opt for a format within the chapter, to keep them interested in reading and not over faced by too much text.

- Make the chapters leave the reader in suspense at the end of one chapter and make them turn that page to the next chapter to find out what happens. Just as in a TV series, they leave you with a cliff hanger, so you are dying to watch the next episode. In other words, your last sentence or paragraph, on each chapter needs to lead them into the next chapter. This is more apparent in a journey book where you want to leave them in suspense at the end of each chapter.

- Even after they have read your book make sure they are motivated to learn more about you and can easily find your website and what other services you have. Remember your book is your calling card, you have much more to offer, after they have read the book and get to meet you in person, take your course, or buy your product, or take a trip with you or.... I have actually had a few people not reach out to me and take a trip with someone else, because they thought I was probably unavailable or too high up for them. Make sure you engage them to your website where you can explain more of what you do. And I don't just mean list your website, if you can go further and offer them some bonus material they can find on your site.

> ❖
>
> At every opportunity the reader could stop, make them read on.
>
> ❖

THE BIGGEST MISTAKE WRITERS MAKE

Procrastination, Confusion, Time Wasting Pitfalls

If there is one piece of knowledge I want to empower you with, it is this. This one important fact is probably the single most powerful tool I can share with you. This problem has caused writers for decades to never write their book or give up halfway through. It has caused frustration in probably 90% of writers, causing them to take months or years longer, than if they had known this one simple secret. So here it is. Writing a book requires different parts of your personality, different parts of your brain to be engaged.

The mistake that almost every writer tries to do, is to use these parts simultaneously. To switch back and forth between these different modes. Not many of us are effective when we are doing this. You would never try to do a sales pitch at work while at the same time keep going back and forth between consoling a child. If you were watching a movie you were really into and in the middle of it, someone kept asking you difficult technical questions about something, you would find it annoying and distracting. You would have to decide to quit one or the other task or you would not be fully present for either. We may think we are good at multi-tasking, and perhaps sometimes we are but not when they require completely opposite sides of your brain.

In writing, I have found that there are three different modes of working, all of which are required (unless you really outsource some). Most writers attempt to do these three modes together, switching back and forth. Because each requires a separate brain flow, it is very difficult to do all these things together or switch quickly back and forth and the end result is frustration.

❖

If you understand this one concept, it will save you months or years of frustration.

❖

These are the 3 distinct modes I have found:

1. ***Core content writing*** – When you are creatively writing, even non-fiction, business or technical writing, you are in a creative mind flow. For many it is difficult to get yourself into this flow, so when it happens, you cannot take yourself away from this. It doesn't matter if you are writing with a pen, typing or recording. This is the most important time to cultivate and I do have some suggestions on getting you into this

space, but once you are there, keep going for as long as you can. This is a very creative right brain activity that almost becomes subliminal or semi-automatic.

2. ***Editing***–There are different forms of editing that I will go through in this book and they take the order of rough editing, editing, line editing and copy editing. I don't include proofreading in these. Editing requires a mixture of creative brain activity and left-brain organizational skills. Here you are reorganizing thoughts and words creatively into aesthetically pleasing sentences but also organizing visually and fixing major grammatical and spelling errors. Your brain is using both sides.

3. ***Proofreading*** – This is a very left brain, no nonsense activity. Some even suggest proofreading backwards. That is, starting from one sentence, proofreading that sentence, and then going backwards one sentence, and proofreading that sentence. The purpose of this is to avoid your creative brain kicking in and drawing you into the meaning of the words. Once your creative mind kicks in you lose your accuracy as you get carried away in the thoughts of the words, not the words themselves. In proofreading you cannot allow yourself to be involved in the content.

So, what is the secret?

Do not mix these modes. It is that simple. Yet almost every writer falls into this trap. Do not start writing your content, then go back over that sentence, editing and rewriting it and even correcting your typos as you go. Do not do this! I know it feels natural, it is not. So how do we avoid this? You need a definite plan and structure that does not allow you to do this. It takes a lot of getting used to, but once you start that creative flow, do not allow yourself to edit. When you are in edit mode you are in edit mode. When you are in creative mode you are in creative mode. I promise you, this will save you months of time and frustration.

MOTIVATE YOUR BUTT TO WRITE

Thinking about where to start and how to start, is probably the single most difficult thing facing an author sitting down to write a book. It can be overwhelming, and not just for first time writers. The first thing we're going to do, is create a structure for your entire book. This is usually fun and it's very easy to be motivated about, because you are looking at the whole picture and this is pretty exciting. The problem comes once we get to the core content writing and the actual flushing out and writing of the chapters.

Find Your Groove

Everyone's style is a little bit different, so you are going to have to figure out what style of motivation works best for you. This is a creative process and so it is important to find out what puts you in that creative zone. I know for me personally, there are certain times that I feel creative and love to write. And then there are certain times that I have no interest. This is part of my personality. Even as a child, if I was asked to clean my bedroom it was always at a time that I wasn't interested, and it was a chore. Then once in a while, I would get this spark of imagination and I'd want to clean out my entire room and take the whole day rearranging and loved it. Then later I'll be asked to clean my room again and again I wouldn't feel like it and I'd do it because I had to. This is my personality; when I am in my creative flow, I can write for hours and days, and when I'm not, I'm not. Your style to motivation may be different.

The Break Style

There have been studies made that a person cannot stare at something without losing concentration for more than 25 minutes. Therefore, some people work 25 minutes concentrating then a ten-minute coffee break, then 25 minutes writing, then a ten-minute break. However, this experiment was done while trying to concentrate on something that was boring and not engaging. Personally, I feel when you are in the flow and engaged, you can work for hours and the last thing I want is regimented breaks.

Avoid Distractions

Distractions are our biggest enemy. I find that you need to arrange long blocks of time when you will not be disturbed. Or if you can work in your own bubble of concentration while surrounded by others that's fine too.

Meditation Preparation

I strongly believe in meditation before-hand. Of course, this may be much more relevant to those writing new-age books where I think inspiration is often divinely guided, even to the point of bringing in your semi-conscious automatic writing. By this I mean something similar to when you are driving a car to a very familiar place, it just almost drives itself and your mind gets out of the way. However, I think anyone can benefit from a few minutes centering yourself to access that creative, intuitive side.

Setting Deadlines

Some people work better under pressure, even if you set the deadline yourself. I have written this as a 30 Day plan chopping it up into 30 sessions each about three hours long. This may help you, as it sets up a deadline. Of course, you can do these as 30 consecutive days or 30 odd days spread out, or may choose to do two of these three-hour sessions in a day. But set yourself a more detailed plan if this helps you. Like Monday through Friday, one session a day starting at 10am. Or assigning actual dates to these days.

Create a Habit

Some people form habits, so if you like this, create a habit of writing. Say every evening after dinner, or every morning at 10am. If habits work for you create a writing habit.

Creative Space

Many people need to bridge the gap from busy mind to creative mind. It is not always possible to go from your daily life to just start writing. Many people need a sort of preparation stage that says, "Now we are going to get into our creative zone." This could be setting up your comfortable space, having a routine of things you need to get out of the way first. Certain actions can be programmed into your brain, where your brain says, "Ok now we are going into creative zone mode."

Combat Writers' Block

When you get so called writers block, the secret is to just write, no matter what. Just start. It doesn't matter if it is total crap. Just start typing anything. You can go back and edit later. It may be horrible, you don't have to keep it, but the point is you need to write to get through this. Writer's block is in the starting. It is over thinking, analyzing, letting our insecurities run amok. Believe me just start typing anything, it works!

Your Comfortable Talking Voice

Make sure you are writing with a comfortable talking voice. If you are trying to write as someone you are not, i.e. a perfect sounding professional, you are going to run out of steam.

> ❖
>
> Follow your heart, your style
>
> ❖

If you are having problems stemming from your style, go to how would you say this to someone as if you are just talking.

If you follow the steps and structure you will have a lot easier time. When you get to the core content, we'll go over some different ways to see what motivates you to write.

More About Editing

I am going to be talking about editing, so here is what I mean.

Rough Editing

This is exactly as it sounds, rough editing. You are not going to concern yourself with details. You can correct the major typos and sentence structure. If you have recorded this you will find many words that have been mis-interpreted by the voice system. So, if you recorded it you need to rough edit while it is fresh in your mind as days later you may have no idea what you were trying to say. In a "how to" book, you can also space out your copy into chunks or blocks of text and some spacing and bullets. You are doing general spacing and formatting.

Copy Editing

I am going to group several forms of editing into one term but normally editing is broken out as follows; editing or general editing followed by line editing, followed by copy editing. If you hire a professional editor or general editor, they will normally look at the overall story, concept or expression of your book. They are looking to see if there is a through line, the characters are developed or in the case of a "how to" book, your personality is conveyed, your voice is clear and it is well laid out in terms of the concepts (not visually). They will often give suggestions, such as, "cut this," "make this flow better," "rewrite this area to be more descriptive," etc. They may slash out sections of your book. A line editor is different, they will go literally line by line, rewriting and restructuring sentences so they flow better, the line is more descriptive in a journal book and of course it is grammatically correct at the same time. A professional line editor would be the one actually rewriting your book and probably would provide you with a red underlined Word Doc so you could track the actual changes they made. A copy editor is going into even more detail, restructuring sentences, making the flow better and fixing most of the grammatical errors and typos. In a "how to" book this is going to include making the copy visually pleasing with bullet points, italics, highlighting and spacing. There may remain some grammatical, punctuation and spelling errors that a proofreading is for.

As I discuss your book and I talk about you doing copy editing, I am going to include you doing all of the above.

Proofreading

Proofreading is a very left-brain activity. While you are proofreading you should not be getting into the story or what you wrote or admiring the flow. This is strictly about catching all those little typos and grammatical errors that are left. You will be very temped to get carried into the content and the meaning and it is hard to resist. You can even try proofreading backwards from the end of the book back, sentence by sentence, so you can't possibly be tempted to get involved in the writing. You are strictly looking for spelling and grammatical errors. You have written it, so your brain will naturally glance over very familiar words and miss some of these corrections, so you have to be super focused and it is best to have someone else look at it too.

30
DAY
PLAN

Structure

It is extremely important to create a structure or outline for your entire book as well as each chapter BEFORE you begin writing. One of the biggest mistakes a writer makes, is to start at chapter one and keep going, and believe me by chapter three, it will be a disaster. I am going to outline some tips that I find useful for creating the structure. Once we get into the core content chapters, this is where your creative juices are going to come in and you will have to find your zone of motivation and creativity. This is the time that so called "writer's block" can happen, but you've got a solution for that, right?

❖

Structure, Blueprint, Road Map – An absolute necessity

❖

To avoid these issues, we are going to work in a structure. The structure is the first few chapters being the copyright notice, the table of contents, the forward, the introduction, and other forwarding text. Then the core content which we are going to spend most of our time discussing, then ending with the author's page and some other information.

I am going to organize the steps in this structure into a 30 Day plan of action. This 30 Day plan is going to be particularly important for those of you who work better with deadlines. I am calling it a 30 Day plan, but

I am actually assigning you the plan broken out into 30 sections. Each section should take you about three hours. You may find that this takes you more than three hours, especially at first, if so, that is ok. And some of you may breeze through it in less time. Now set your schedule. You may set yourself 30 consecutive days, doing one three-hour session per day. You may set yourself certain days, such as Monday through Friday, one session per day. Or Saturdays and Sundays only, but doing three sessions per day. Or you may just decide to leave it as 30 sections to be completed as you feel the urge, doing as many sessions as you can complete each day while you are in the creative flow. It is important to finish an entire section before moving on. Don't do half an assignment. Meaning don't do half a chapter. So, if you finish one section, on one day and wish to do another section, make sure you are going to finish that second section. If you are someone that works better on deadlines, I suggest that you mark in your calendar with each of these 30 sections and give yourself an actual time and day to complete the section.

30 Day Summary

Here is the summary of the 30 Day Plan. Continue reading for details.

Day 1

- Mind dump.
- Research other similar books.
- 10-15 groups of ideas.

Day 2

- Draft Chapters using sticky notes.
- Arrange sticky notes into your chapter flow.
- Transfer to computer Word Docs.
- Decide if chapters will have a format within the chapter.

Day 3 – Day 16 (14 days)

- Core Content Writing
- Choose a chapter and do Core Content writing for that chapter (any order).
- Do a rough speed draft of the chapter you chose (can be recorded).
- Follow by a rough edit of that chapter, while it is fresh in your mind.
- Repeat for each chapter (you will have 10-20 chapters) I have assigned 14 days/ 14 sessions which is approximately one chapter per day. Figure out how many chapters you have and if there is more than one chapter per day, decide which chapters are short and you can do two in a day. Remember you don't have to do the chapters in order, so you can decide now which chapters to do on which day or you can just know that you are going to complete any one or two chapters each day. I recommend making sure you complete the entire chapter once you start a chapter, don't do half a chapter.

Day 17- Day 23 (7 days)

- Copyedit each chapter, through entire book.
  For this I recommend starting at the beginning of the book and going through in order of chapters to the end. I have allocated seven days, which is approximately two chapters per day. Once you start a chapter though, be sure to finish that chapter. You have already done a rough draft of each chapter immediately after you wrote or recorded that chapter while it was fresh in your mind. Now we are going in order of chapters and spending more time tweaking and arranging your text. Don't worry too much about spelling and grammar you are going to do a proof reading at the end. Just change the glaring errors and arrange the paragraphs and bullet points.

Day 24

- Transfer all chapters into one master Word Doc and add page numbers.
- Tie the chapters together.
- Make the chapter titles exciting.
- Add forward and after pieces.

Day 25 – Day 27 (3 days)

- Proofread yourself.
- I have assigned 3 days/3 sessions, so you can get through ⅓ of your book each day.

- Ask friends to proofread.
- Send out for professional proofreading

Day 28

- Get your ISBN number.
- Finalize your book title.
- Send out for layout.
- Create cover ideas and text, send to your designer.

Day 29

- You may have to wait a few days to get your layout and cover back from your designer
- Make any final changes.
- Upload your book to Amazon for print and kindle.
- You will need to wait up to 72 hours for your book to appear.

Day 30

- Now it is time to market.
- Create your free book promotion.
- Create your social media campaigns.
- Create your email campaigns.
- Create your paid Amazon ad campaigns.
- Make your book a Best Seller.

DAY 1

Mind Dump

This is the time when you are just going to write ideas, concepts, thoughts, and one-liners and buzz words that relate to your concept and what you might include in your book. This is a sheet of paper of random ideas or a Mind Dump. I like to do this on a big sheet of scrap paper with a pen. Other people like to do this on a whiteboard. There are now computer programs specifically for authors and they include a space for this type of note blasting. Personally, at this stage, I like the old-fashioned way with paper and pen. If this is a "how to" book you are going to write various concepts you want to explain, not in any particular order and random thoughts you might work into your book. If it is a journal book following a timeline, you may be jotting down particular events as well as thoughts and feeling and they probably will not come out in the order of time.

Research

You might want to research other books in your genre and see what points they covered. It may remind you of some concept you forgot to include in your book. If so, add these notes to your Mind Dump paper.

10-15 Groups of Ideas

On the same piece of paper or on a second piece of paper, group your ideas into groups of 10 to 15 blocks of ideas. These are going to be the early drafts to possibly become chapters. Ultimately, you may delete some of the ideas. A block of words or ideas may become a chapter as envisioned, however, some ideas may be expanded and spread over two or three chapters and some of the ideas may be shortened and several merged into one chapter. If anyone was to see this piece of paper at this point they would think you had gone mad. It is not supposed to be pretty.

DAY 2

Draft Chapters on Sticky Notes

Once you have the 10 to 15 ideas, we are going to create possible chapters. At this stage I personally like to use either index cards or sticky notes. Again, there are computer programs, like Scrivener.com particularly for authors and it has features that will help you do this. Alternatively, you could create these idea groupings or draft chapters on a Word Doc. I prefer to have them physical where I can move them around, but I'm a little bit old school.

Don't worry, these can be changed later and probably will be. You may find you need to add a couple more sticky notes for new ideas that you forgot to include.

On each sticky note write a temporary chapter title. Then under the title, write words and sentences that are concepts you would include in this temporary chapter. The content for each chapter should be approximately the same length. Aim to end up with between 10 and 20 chapters, so between 10 and 20 sticky notes. Personally, I prefer more short chapters than long ones, so the reader feels they finished another learning block quicker and is more enthused to read on to another chapter. Once your ideas for each chapter are flushed out, these ideas should result in chapters that will eventually be each about 5-7 pages.

Arrange Sticky Notes into Chapter Flow

Now is the time to study these temporary chapters and rearrange them into the order you think they should flow. You may also decide that you want to merge two sticky notes together into one chapter and you may decide to split some sticky notes into more than one chapter and expand on them. Each chapter may contain a group of ideas, perhaps an example and an answer.

Journal style books that have a timeline, or a diary type book, are slightly easier as you will be mostly going in the order of time. However, you still want to group important events into sticky notes. Even though you may be going in order of time, some events will be very quick, while some events will be spread over several chapters and you will need to determine this.

In a journey book, the sticky notes are probably going to run in sequence of time. However, you may decide to rearrange these and to do flashbacks of certain events. In particular, the first chapter needs to really grab your attention, so perhaps the first chapter may be something more exciting in the journey that gives you a glimpse of the future and it's not within the timeline. In a "how to" type book the first chapter may explain exactly what you are going to learn in this book, to create anticipation of why they want to read it. The first chapter may also be a short life story with impact to motivate the reader to read on.

Transfer to a Word Doc

Now that you have a good idea of each chapter and the basic concepts and you have a chapter order or flowchart, this is a good time to transfer this to your computer, if you haven't already. If you don't have a publishing program, Word Doc or Google Docs will work just fine. If you are planning to voice record some of this book, it is best to work on Google Docs. Afterwards you can transfer from Google Docs to Word Docs if you prefer. I create a new folder for the book and within it, one Word doc for each chapter. Each chapter should now include the working title of the chapter and some notes about the content within that chapter. You can label these documents Ch1, Ch2, Ch3 etc. so that they will list in sequence order in your computer. Later when you add preview material, such as a Copyright Notice page, a Forward, and a Table of Contents page, you can label these A1, A2, A3 etc. so they come before the core chapters. When you add sections at the back of the book such as an authors page, reference information etc. you can label these Z1, Z2, Z3. A program like Scrivener.com will organize this better for you.

Chapter Format

You will find some books work very well that have a format within the chapter. Meaning each chapter will follow the exact same format except for the beginning pre-chapters and ending informational chapters. For instance, each chapter could take a problem and give a solution. A format could be, the problem, the solution, an explanation of the solution, a list of the items needed to be resolved, an example, and then a chapter summary. Each chapter would follow that same format. It could be a collection of true- life stories, each chapter being a story. Formatting a chapter is appealing to the reader as they become adjusted to the format and know what they are to expect. However, you may find if you adhere to this very strictly, some chapters may take a lot of extra work to make it fit your format. You may decide though to have one element of formatting only. Perhaps each chapter has a summary at the end of what you should have learned in the chapter or perhaps each chapter has an example that is separated by a box. Or perhaps each chapter has a quote from a famous person that emphasizes your chapter lesson. If you are including a chapter format, you will now need to make notes within you draft chapter documents to form the chapter structure.

DAY 3-DAY 16 (14 DAYS)

Core Content Writing – Fill in the Chapters

This is the area that a lot of people feel over faced or fall into writer's block. This is the creative writing phase, so you need to figure out what best motivates you and creates that mind set for you to write. Read the notes before about motivation and getting into your creative zone.

Now choose the chapter that you are going to work on first. It absolutely does not need to be the first chapter followed by the second chapter etc. Choose the chapter you are most excited about. You have each chapter already outlined, so you can go in any order you like. At the end we will tweak them to make sure they flow from one chapter to the next.

Now get yourself really comfortable in a place where you know you will not be disturbed. I highly recommend a few minutes of meditation before you start to center yourself and if you have some kind of ritual, such as clearing your desk or making snack, that is great too.

Choose one chapter that you will work on. You can always add a second chapter but for now we will dedicate ourselves to one.

I have assigned 14 days to do the speed reading and rough draft on each chapter. This may be one chapter

❖

PLACE HOLDER TIP – There are going to be times when you need a place holder to come back to. Either you need to look something up, you can't remember the name of something, or you simply need to come back to this place to rewrite something. Here place the letters tk. This is because tk is not used in English language words so you can do a search for tk and see all your place holders. If you have difficulty getting the voice program to recognize this, use a word you are not using in the rest of your book, for the same purpose. Like the word "zoo" or "Fred." If you are voice recording this, make sure your place holder is being transcribed correctly.

❖

per day, or it may mean more than one chapter on some days, depending on how many chapters your book has.

Rough Speed Draft can be Recorded

Now that you have chosen the chapter, you should already have the notes about that chapter content, so now it is about flushing out that content and putting that into words. Now we are going to write this first draft of this chapter as fast as you can. Yes, you heard me, AS FAST AS YOU CAN.

If you like you can do this by recording it. Recording it is wonderful as it is very fast. You will spend extra time on the back end editing it and making sense of some of the things that are not picked up by the recording correctly, but if you get used to this it will save you a lot of time.

Dragon Naturally Speaking is a great voice translator tool for authors, and it is very accurate, but it costs around $700. It actually learns your voice over time to become even more accurate. But to start, Google Docs works perfectly well. Just open up a Google Doc and under "tools" you will find voice type capabilities. You simply speak into your computer mic and it will transcribe your voice onto the page. You can say "new paragraph" and it will create a new paragraph. It will take a little getting used to, but it actually works really well. VERY IMPORTANT, do not be tempted to look at all the mistakes and don't try to fix it yet. Don't stop, don't edit, just keep talking.

If you have decided just to type this, then start typing your thoughts as fast as you can. Go super speed and try not to stop too much. The trick is just to keep going fast. You may be thinking you are not being articulate, or you are repeating yourself, or it is not phased correctly, don't worry, keep going, this is about speed. Stopping to correct errors will switch your brain flow. Don't interrupt your flow.

❖

FONT TIP –At this point I would use whatever standard type font you already have in your Word Docs as long as it is easily readable. At the end, your graphic designer is going to convert all the text into the font you decide as the layout is created.

❖

If you have to look back at your notes to see what other content you are going to write in this chapter that's ok, but DO NOT edit, just continue on without editing. Keep going until you have written a rough draft of your entire chapter.

Rough Edit That Chapter

Now you are allowed to go back and do a rough edit of the chapter you just wrote at speed. It does not have to be perfect at this stage, but you can correct the major typos and sentence structure. If you have recorded this you will find many words that have been mis-interpreted by the voice system. It should be still fresh in your mind and so you should know what you meant to say. This is why I am going to let you go back now and edit. If you leave this for several days, you may not remember what you were saying or thinking.

You can also do a small amount of spacing and bullets, doing your general spacing and formatting within the chapter. Remember if you are a "how to" book, you need to put in lots of lists, spaces and text that will be boxed out and lots of spacing. You don't need to tweak the entire format here, but you can do a rough draft on what ideas are spaced together or put into bullets. So, chop your text into blocks with lots of spaces.

❖

Sit back and congratulate yourself your book is now complete, now we are going to tweak and edit but the core content is there!

❖

Don't worry you are going to come back and do a much more thorough edit.

NEXT DAY

Next Chapter Core Content & Rough Edit

You are going to do one or two chapters per day. Remember to do the speed writing and then the rough edit on the chapter before moving on to the next chapter.

Now choose the next chapter you would like to do and remember it doesn't have to be in order. Again, start with writing your core content in a very fast draft, recorded or written. Then when completely finished, you can do the rough chapter edit. Go back and fix the major errors. You can start some of the spacing, lists and making the spacing of the text look interesting. This chapter should be about the same length as the previous one you just did but you don't need to be too strict about that.

NEXT DAY

Each Chapter Core Content & Rough Edit

Now move to the next chapter that you choose and repeat.

Do each chapter until you have flushed out all the core content chapters.

DAY 17 – DAY 23 (7 DAYS)

Copyedit All Chapters

Now is the fun part. This stage I am going to call copyediting. Go through each chapter. I prefer to start at the beginning of the book and go start to finish. I have assigned 7 days for this portion which is going to be approximately 2 chapters a day, sometimes 3 chapters a day.

For each chapter, tweak the copy and arrange it into interesting blocks. You can fix any typos that you see that jump out, but don't be too concerned. At the end you will do a proof edit to catch all those little nuances. If you are looking for typos and grammatical errors at this point, it will take you out of the creative flow and put you in a different mind-set. You are copyediting. Actually, this may be called simply editing or line editing. Different terms are used for different stages.

You may want to expand some thoughts. You may want to slash and cut chunks of copy. Then start to organize the design and separate blocks of ideas.

You may want to highlight sentences that you want your designer to reprint as a block of copy in your design.

If you are writing a journey book, you are going to be doing copyediting a little differently and spending much more time here, writing and tweaking sentences. A journey book needs to flow grammatically, and creatively, much more than a "how to" book and may take you considerably longer. You are going to be tweaking the flow of your sentences. You may expand, go deeper, going into more detail. Think, what did it look like, feel like, smell like? Describe in more detail and enhance your sentences to be as descriptive as possible.

If you are writing a journey book and are really having a difficult time, this could be a point that you hire a professional copyeditor, but give it your best shot before you call in a professional as most people really don't need it. These may be called editors, line editors or copy editors. Generally, an editor will help you with the overall

❖

TIP – If you wish your graphic designer to highlight or repeat a sentence again in a highlighted block somewhere in that chapter, there will not be an indication that this line of copy is "floating text." You can highlight these odd blurbs to let your graphic designer know this copy is "floating copy," to insert wherever it looks pleasing in the design.

❖

structure of a book and direct you on how to rewrite it. A line editor will go through line by line and help you to restructure awkward sentences and a copy editor is getting more into the grammar. If you hire an editor be sure to talk to them about what your needs are regardless of their title. For a "how to" book I really feel you don't need one.

Copyediting is very different to proofreading. Writing core content, copyediting, and proof-reading are three completely different activities which require a switch of your brain flow, so do not switch back and forth. Proofreading comes at the end and you will be specifically looking for spelling and grammar errors, right now you are just changing glaring errors that you happen to see.

DAY 24

Tie Chapters Together & Make Chapter Headers Exciting

At this point I would transfer all the chapters to one large document and add page numbers at the bottom, so you will start to see how close your page number is to your desired amount (remember the number of pages on a Word Doc is going to turn out to be more than double the pages once it is printed).

This stage is really fun as you now have almost a full book and you are just tweaking it to make it exciting.

Make sure you love the chapter titles. A title should grab a person and make them want to read that chapter. It can be seductive, secretive, and alluring but it should most of all peak the readers interest. If the titles don't grab you, then edit the title. If, however your book is strictly a "how to" step by step practical guide, your titles should be clear and simple. Enticing the reader to keep going to collect the next piece of information or the next step.

❖

TIP–You are working on a word doc page, so you will be temped to correct the spacing so that a header is not left on the bottom of the page but moved to the top of the next page. Don't do this. Remember when it is laid out, your book size is very different, so the text is not going to be on the same page. So, ignore the page breaks where a title is cut off from the text, otherwise when you come to laying out the book, you or your graphic artist are going to end up with extra spaces in places and have to fix it all. Starting a new page for a new chapter is fine if you prefer to do that, as your designer is going to move chapter headers anyway.

❖

Now we also want to make sure that chapters flow from the end of one to the next. This is much more important in a journey book but is somewhat important in a "how to" book. The idea is to get the reader to read the next chapter. In a journey book, you can often write a sentence at the end of the chapter to get the person to turn the page. Write something that alludes that there is suspense and they need to keep reading because there is something new about to be revealed, a hook or a surprise coming in the next chapter. That, coupled with a great next chapter title to get them to read on will make your book a page-turner. There might not be as much opportunity to do this in a "how to" book. Sometimes a chapter summary of what they have learned is motivation to go forward and accomplish another block of learning.

Add Forward and After Book Pieces

Now you are going to add in the extra bits and pieces. I suggest you create separate Word Docs for each additional section. Here are main sections you may decide to use:

❖

TIP–don't do this until you are sure you have all the final names of your chapters, otherwise if you keep changing them you will have to keep changing this list.

❖

Copyright disclaimer – Check out other books and rewrite for yours

Book title page – Don't worry about the blank pages and the page with the title, your art designer will do this when they are doing the book layout.

Table of Contents – Make a list of chapter titles and titles of other bits. Don't put in page numbers. This will be done at the time the book is laid out by the art designer.

Forward – If you have someone of some notoriety that will say a few words about your book that is great. Put that here.

Introduction – This could be your story of how you got into this.

What you will learn from this book – If this is a "how to" book, layout clear bullet points of what they expect to learn.

Praise for this book – If you had some reviews done at this point. Most of you will not.

Book Core Content Chapters

Acknowledgement – this is the thankyou page. This can be done at the beginning or the end. I would say put it at the end unless you are thanking someone well known who endorses your book.

Authors Page – your page, some personal info and where they find you.

Upsell – more about you and your products.

Indexing – Indexing is more common in certain information books. This is where you would have a list of words that a person might look up that appear in your book, next to the page numbers where they appear. For instance, in a crystals and minerals book you might have in the index, Amethyst- pg 23,45,118, meaning Amethyst crystals are mentioned on these pages. This is a very tedious job and I would only do for rich information books. Personally, I would send this out for a professional to do.

DAY 25 - DAY 27 (3 DAYS)

Proofread Yourself

As I discussed earlier, creative writing your core content, copyediting, and proofreading are three entirely different brain flows. They require a different type of mind set and this is why I am recommending that you do one at a time. Now you are down to proofreading. You can let a professional do the proofreading, but I recommend you do your own pass first and then have a professional do another pass. Your brain automatically glosses over words that are familiar to you and even words with jumbled letters, so this requires concentration.

Some people recommend starting at the back of the book and working backwards, one sentence at a time. Perhaps using a ruler under each line to keep your eyes focused. This is so you are not becoming engaged in your story and getting back into creative mode or even copyediting mode, you are strictly looking for spelling and grammatical errors. Any switch into thought of the book content will stop your concentration.

I have assigned 3 days/3 sessions, so you can get through ⅓ of your book each day

Send Out for Proofreading

Ask some trusted friends to read it. Although they are not professional, a second set of eyes is useful, and they will often catch issues you may have missed.

It is good to have a professional do a final proofread, unless you are really confident and extra ordinarily detail oriented. A recommendation for a proofreader is always the best as there can be a huge difference in the quality of the work. There are sites where you can find a lot of freelancers such as upwork.com or fiverr.com Make sure you ask for samples if you didn't get a recommendation. You may also have to tell them how far you want to go. Your book may use colloquial language and display your personality and you may get an editor who changes these things into a more grammatically correct format, but then you lose your feel or personality. So, tell them how far you want them to go. Usually they will do this via Word Doc or Google Docs where you can see the red underline of the changes they have made. They usually charge by the page or word count. This will normally cost you between $200 and $500.

Choose Your Title

Now it's time to take your working title and create a best seller title. A title is incredibly important, so you want to give this a lot of thought.

Good titles often include:

- It should be powerful enough to create an emotional response

- It should answer what's in it for me? What am I going to get out of reading this?

- It should include popular searchable key words in your field

- It should accurately portray the content of your book

- It should be easy to pronounce

- It should be easy to remember

- If appropriate include a number or length of time

Title and Subtitle

It doesn't always follow this rule, but a good title usually contains a catchy title, followed by a sub-title which is more descriptive about the subject. So, if the main title doesn't explain what the book is, the subtitle will contain the explanation.

Here are some examples of my book titles and subtitles:

- *What's up With My Life? Finding and Living Your True Purpose*

- *30 Days to Prosperity: a Workbook to Manifest Abundance*

- *Running with Wolves: a Woman's Memoir of Sex Scandal and Seduction*
- *How to Talk to Your Pets: Animal Communication for Dogs, Cats & Other Critters*

If it is not clear what form your book is, you could include in the subtitle, "a memoir," "a true-life story," "a workbook," "my journey," "how to" etc. if it is not already clear from the title. You don't want someone wondering if it is a novel.

You want to have great searchable key words in your descriptive subtitle.

Numbers and dates

If it fits for you to put a number, such as;

- 7 Ways to…
- 9 Steps to…
- 10 Things you Need to Know to…

Numbers work really well for "how to" books, especially 7, 9 and 10. This is because the reader knows they have a plan and steps to accomplish something in. There is some research that says odd numbers work well (3,5,7,9) as well as the number 10. More than ten and it sounds like more steps than they are willing to take on. Although 101 ideas, 101 ways to… works for something you are bringing to someone, as opposed to steps they need to take.

Timelines and days, work great too, such as;

- Lose weight in 3 months
- Ace your exams in 5 weeks
- 30 Days to Write your Book

The reason this is popular is, the reader knows exactly how long it will take them to learn and be able to reach their end goal. Non-fiction "how to" readers value their time and want to know exactly what they will get and how long will that take. Of course, they want to accomplish it quickly.

Existing Title

Title cannot be copywritten. This means that you can have a title for your book, even if that title already exists. Of course, it is not preferable to have the same title but if you are really in love with the title and the other book is not a huge seller then it is not totally out of the question.

Popular Searched Key Words

You need to have searchable key words, if not in your main title, certainly in your subtitle. To do this go to Google Trends or Google Ad words and see what are the most popular search terms for your subject. Test about 10 or 15 words associated with your subject to see which words or terms are most often searched for.

You want to try to get some of the top searched words in your title and include those terms as well as other highly searched terms in your book description.

For instance, for my book, *30 Days to Prosperity: a Workbook to Manifest Abundance*

I would search terms such as Manifest, Manifesting, Prosperity, Abundance, Rich, Money, Law of Attraction, Wealth, Happiness. I would try to create a title from the highest searched terms. Those that don't make it into your title, can be used in your description. I would try to put all those and any other well searched terms in the description of my book on my back cover and the Amazon description.

The program publisherrocket.com has a built-in feature that helps you find the top search key words for your book.

As you can see for this title "30 Days to Prosperity: a Workbook to Manifest Abundance"

I was able to include

- A time they can complete – 30 days
- What's in it for them – prosperity, abundance
- Highly searched key words in this genre – prosperity, manifest, abundance
- Define what kind of book it is – a workbook
- Evoke an emotional response – most people respond emotionally to thinking about abundance

Send out for Layout

Unless you are truly versed in graphic design, I recommend you send your book to a professional to lay it out. This is the interior design of your book. There are programs to do this yourself, but this must look professional. If not, and it looks a little off, this will mark your book as "amateurish" and immediately discredit you and even the subject matter of your book. Remember this is your calling card. The content can be great but if it is laid out poorly it will reflect on the value of your content and the value of you. Still, if you are sure it will look professional if you do it yourself, go ahead. You can find a graphic designer, ones recommended are best, but you can also find at upwork.com and fiverr.com but ask for samples of their work. This may be the same person who you hire to layout your cover. The layout will cost you on average $500 ($200-$700). The cover will cost you around $500 to $1000. You can probably make a deal with the designer to do both.

Graphic design involves laying the book out;

- Use a simple type font that is easy to read.

- You can do something a little fancier for the chapter headers and perhaps a graphic but make sure even your design fonts for the headers are still easily readable.

- "How to" books and Journey books will have very different layouts. "How to" books should be very visually appealing with a lots of design, but a journey book will look almost the same as a novel.

- For a "how to" book, you want your graphic designer to have a field day with creativity and make your book look visually interesting. This can be done with bullets, lists, spaces, italics, bold copy, boxed out copy, highlighted boxes of copy, and diagrams. Consider having a space for the reader to make notes if this is appropriate. Interesting design is extremely important for "how to" books. For journal, time-line books, you may just need a few deign tweaks to give it more visual appeal. This could be an occasional sentence highlighted in a block, and a nicer looking graphic or font for the chapter header.

- You may want to have a chapter format design, such as a summary at the end of each chapter in a box. Or you might have a running graphic. "How to" books need to be very interesting, visually.

- I am presuming if you have inside images they will be black and white. If they are color it is recommended that they are in the same "fold" and not spread out, so you only have to print a certain number of pages in color. This will depend on the publisher. Color is way more expensive

- Page breaks–your graphic designer can make recommendations on where to put blank pages, if any. If you have a blank page between chapters for instance, if you always start a chapter on the left side, always on the right side or if it can alternate. Do you always leave a blank page to start a chapter? How much space your chapter header takes up. This may also be determined by your page count. If you have a lot of pages you may want to skip page breaks. If you have too little pages you will want to spread out your design to fill up more pages.

- Let the graphic designer know what you like for the page header and footer; if you want the book title and author name as a header and footer on alternating pages, or the chapter name and author name, and where you like the page number. Look at other book examples to see what you like.

- Table of contents – usually the graphic designer will write the page number next to each chapter title (you left the page number off and just a list of headers), this is because the page number is not going to be final until you have passed off on the layout.

Size of Your book

You will need to determine the size of your book before you send to your designer. Size definitely does matter! There are standard Amazon sizes (which also differ for white or cream pages). In Amazon if you stick to a standard size you can be included in the extended book distribution for your print book. Extended distribution means bookstores like Barnes and Noble and bookstands at airports would be able to pick up your book. That would be wonderful! Whether they really do, is probably rare, but its worth a shot. To do this you need to stick to Amazon's standard sizing. However, there may be times that you specifically want an over sized book or a smaller size book. I did my Reiki Manuals in large format and my "30 Days to Prosperity" book, in a different almost large square format, because it was a workshop book that people could write in. I also made some mini "pocket" books, based on the idea that people would like a series of one-subject small books. On these small ones, Amazon wouldn't even print them as small as I wanted, so I had them printed at a different source (lightningsource.com) and although I published these on Amazon, the version on Amazon is a slightly larger size. This slightly larger size on Amazon was one of Amazon's selections however it was not included in their standard sizing for extended distribution.

You will also have a choice of white or cream paper. This is a personal choice. I prefer white paper generally, especially for "how to" books. I did some select "Prosperity Classics," based on books from the early 1900's, in cream as I felt this was more in keeping with this antique style.

❖

Size definitely does matter!

❖

Some standard sizes on Amazon for extended distribution are available in white and not cream paper.

These are standard sizes in inches, width x height. These can be on white or cream paper except where noted. There are more sizes, check **kdp.amazon.com** for complete list;

- 5 x 8
- 5.06 x 7.81 not cream paper, only white paper
- 5.25 x 8
- 5.5 x 8.5
- 6 x 9
- 7 x 10 not cream paper, only white paper

Kindle Version

The graphic designer who lays out your print book, may design your kindle version layout as well, but these may look quite different. There are programs now that make it easier than before to create your own ebook format, but still this can be quite complicated, especially if you have a lot of graphics or images in your book. You may have added a lot of design features, graphics and bullets for a "how to" book. You do want to keep these for your kindle version, but they may be a little more complicated to translate correctly and this is why I recommend getting a pro.

Here is a reason the pages and layout will be different. If you are looking to put your book in the kindle unlimited program (kdp select) where readers can read unlimited kindle books, which I would recommend, you are going to get paid per page. You get paid for the amount of pages the person reads. Unless Amazon has changed their programming, which they may well do, even if a person skips to the last page and goes direct to page 300, you get paid as if the reader read every page up to 300. Some unscrupulous authors realized this and started writing books that were 1000 pages long, and on the first page asked customers to "click here" for some secret or reward at the back of the book. This would take the reader to the last page of the book for some secret or reward. These authors even went as far as publishing 3000 page books with content so spread out or repeated over and over that they were really not books at all. I am not suggesting you do this. But I am suggesting that a nice long layout is not a bad thing in the kindle version. And also, a reason for them to click towards the end of the book is also not a bad thing. Again, Amazon may have caught this loop-hole and changed this. Giving the person great content that makes them read the entire book is really our goal. But if you have condensed the pages for print you can now expand them for kindle.

Also, in your kindle version you can use clickable links. Don't put too many links so your book becomes a bunch of links and looks like an advertisement. But you should for sure put a link for people to be able to reach you or buy the product you are talking about in the book, both at the front of the book and at the back of the book. You might want to think of doing a link to free bonus material from your kindle book to your website. This is great as long as you really do give them bonus content.

In your print book you can include your website too, but in print don't include complicated links. In print, the easier it is for the reader to remember your link and type it in later, the better. If the link is too complicated, the reader won't remember it and they will have a hard time even typing it in.

We will get more into what platforms you should use later but for Kindle you are going to need to have your Kindle book in .mobi form. If you are going to be using it on other platforms you may want a second version from your graphic designer in epub format.

Of course, the size of your book does not matter in your kindle version, so normally your print file will be produced first and then your graphic designer will best adapt that into a kindle .mobi file. And again, remember on the kindle unlimited you are being paid per page read.

Write Your Cover Blurbs

I do not advocate doing the cover yourself, but you will need to write the cover blurb for the back and any lines of copy you want on the front of the book. You can look at other books to see how much copy you can comfortably fit, but generally less is more. You want the minimum copy that says everything you need to say. With less copy your text can be bigger. If it is a "how to" book, outline the important bullet points of what you will learn on your back cover. Work on cutting down the words to say what you mean with the least amount of words. You may want a few blurbs on the front cover, but I would limit the words on the front.

Include the searchable keywords you discovered when you were researching to decide on your title. Now you can include all the additional highly searched terms that you didn't get to use in your title.

Your description should include:

- What's in it for the reader- what they are going to get from reading this.
- How your book is going to make something easier, faster or better for the reader.

- What is special and unique about your book that is not in other books.

- The secrets you are going to reveal.

- How long it will take someone to accomplish what your book offers.

- How this book is going to change the readers life.

- Bullet points on what they will learn through this book.

- If anyone famous or brilliant is doing what you say in this book.

Best Selling Cover

You can write the most interesting book in the world, but if your cover looks unappealing or unprofessional, your book is dead in the water, no one is even going to get to read it. Unless you are a competent graphic designer and have some experience designing books, I would not even dream of doing your own book cover. A good designer will add little touches like drop shadows on the title and believe me this attention to detail is going to make a huge difference.

It is of course great to have an idea of what you want, perhaps where on the page you like your author name, some color schemes you like, some graphics or photo ideas. Make copies of other book covers as examples so you can say "I like this header from this one, and a simple image like this one, and I prefer the way this book has the copy on the back."

The images or photos are extremely important. If you are providing an image, make sure it is high enough quality and resolution (preferably 1Meg or greater). I find the graphic designers are great at finding images. Make sure you have the copyright to use an image. Your graphic designer probably knows where to find stock images and you will need to pay a small copyright fee if you use these. Normally about $50. Such photo stock agencies include Shutterstock.com and istockphoto.com

Here are some important things to keep in mind:

- Make your cover design clean and clear
- Use bright colors with simple designs that pop
- Make an easy to read title and graphics
- Don't over complicate the image
- Make the back-cover text easy to read
- Make sure you have the rights to use any images

You may see people posting on Facebook, "What do you think about this cover or that?" In reality, they are probably not really looking for an opinion, rather pretending to want your opinion but really just letting you know they have a book coming out. Plus, people like to give their opinion and when they do, they feel like they have a stake in the game and want to buy your book. Not a bad ploy.

DAY 28

ISBN

You will need an ISBN code for your book. This is a unique tracking code for your book. It is a 13 digit number and has a corresponding graphic of uniquely sized vertical lines (a barcode). Amazon gives you the option to give you one for free as you upload your book. However, if you want to sell the book yourself in shops you would need to get your own, so some people prefer to buy their own. You can get one of these at Bowker, myidentifiers.com

The cost is around $125, or if you buy 10 they go down to about $30 each. Sometimes your designer may be able to sell you one cheaper if they bought a bulk pack. You will need to register the name of your book and the author to that ISBN. Technically if you

❖

TIP–When you upload your own ISBN in Amazon, it asks you for the "imprint." This means the "publisher" that you registered at myidentifiers. com and it must be exactly the same, or it will tell you it doesn't match.

❖

have different version, say a version of a different size or with edited additions or translated into a different language, you need a separate ISBN for each. There is some optional information which it may ask you to add as you register the ISBN. If it is optional, I don't bother.

You don't need an ISBN for a kindle book, you just need it for your print book. The Kindle book is assigned a different number by Amazon for the Kindle version. You will also have the opportunity to link your print and kindle versions of the same book by linking the ISBN number.

As you upload your print book, Amazon will automatically add the barcode which is the graphic of the ISBN number. If you are selling your book separately in bookstores you will need to get a barcode as well. You can buy a bar code at the same place you get your ISBN. This is the graphic for your ISBN (the block of lines you see on the back of a book that the bookstore scans for the price). You don't need this for Amazon as it will auto load this for you. Your designer will leave a space on your cover where Amazon will add the bar code, or you can get your own bar code and your designer will place it on the back cover.

Congratulations!

Congratulations! You now have a pdf file from your art designer of your final layout and you also have a cover file. You should also have your .mobi file for kindle and perhaps an epub file for others.

Do I need to File for Copyright?

By copyright law, you automatically own the copyright the moment you start writing your book without filing anything. So, you don't need to file for a copyright, but you can do this to give you more security down the line. You can file your copyright with the copyright office at copyright.gov There is a charge. I believe the normal filing charge is $65, or if you are just registering a single book and you are the only author then $45. You receive a temporary filing certificate to say you applied and then presuming everything is ok, you will receive the actual copyright certificate 3-6 months later.

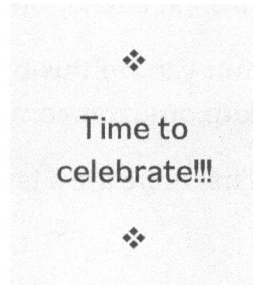

❖

Time to celebrate!!!

❖

You only need the actual copyright certificate if you decided to bring a copyright lawsuit against someone. But you are not penalized if you do this copyright filing after the fact, as you are still the copyright holder as soon as you write it.

DAY 29

Self-Publishing on Amazon

You are now ready to upload your book to Amazon for print and to kindle for your e-book version.

You can do this by going to Kindle Direct Publishing: **kdp.amazon.com**

First there are a few things you need to know:

Categories

You can place your book in two categories. Categories are extremely important. I can't stress this enough. This is because it helps readers search and find you, but far more important is how it can help you become a "Best Seller." Amazon gives a best seller denomination overall which is extremely hard to get, but more importantly Amazon gives a "Best Seller," label within the category that you are in.

You will be asked to select categories for your print book as you upload it and again for your kindle version upload. The categories that you can choose from are slightly different between kindle and print.

So, let's say your book is in the category of Business. This is a difficult category to stand out in, as you are competing against books like "Rich Dad, Poor Dad." To become number one in this category would take you a ton more sales. Let's say that same book could fit in the category of business accounting, where there are not as many books in this category. To become a best seller in this accounting category, may only take 6 book sales. I will go into exactly how to do this, but you need to know now, that you need to pick the two categories as the most obscure, easiest category for you to rank highest in, that still fits your book. You are obviously not allowed to put your book in Arabic Women Studies, if it is about bitcoin.

The program publisherrocket.com will help you find categories that are the easiest for your book to become a best seller in. As you search categories for your topic, this program shows you which books are number one in that category and how many book sales it took them to get to that.

❖

Look for unpopular categories that fit your book.

❖

You want to choose a category where it took them the least number of book sales to be number one.

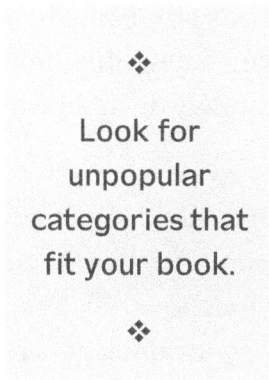

Key Words

Key words on Amazon will help someone find your book when they are searching. Yes, these are important, but nowhere near as important as the category. Publisherrocket.com will help you find good key words.

You also researched key words when you were creating your book title and description, so you should already have a list. You can choose 7 key words.

Extended Distribution

There is little downside to enrolling in this program. This is where Amazon allows book shops, like airport shelves to pick up your book. Of course, you could do this yourself if you had the time to dedicate to this, and maybe make a few pennies more, but again, this is not our goal. Our goal is to get as many books out as possible, so enroll. This is where the book size and page color comes into play, as it must fit the more standard sizes or it can't be included in this program. Of course, you knew this before you created the layout, so you already decided whether you want your book included.

Kindle Unlimited

The KDP select program is where if you enroll your book, Amazon Kindle unlimited subscribers get to read your book for free. You get paid on how many pages of your book gets read. Amazon pays you a share from a pool of money from these subscribers. The exact amount varies, but it is around a penny a page. So, you are getting $2-3 if someone reads your book completely. Remember where I talked about the cheaters that create 3,000 page fake books and tell them to turn to the back of the book so the system counts 3,000 pages read? Probably a loophole that will be closed soon. Anyway, yes you want to enroll! You will probably find that you make almost as much income through this program as you do on your print book sales through Amazon. Plus, what is your purpose? To get as many people reading your book as possible because these are your potential clients, so you want to encourage your book to be read.

In order to be in Kindle Unlimited, you need to dedicate your kindle book exclusively to Amazon. That means you can't also publish on BarnesandNoble.com or other platforms. My personal opinion is Amazon is king, it's not worth the effort of going to all the other platforms, go ahead and give Amazon exclusive. This also gives you the right to do free book promotions, which you want to do, and I'll get into that when we talk about marketing. The exclusive period is for three months, after which you can opt out of the program or if you don't opt out, it will keep renewing for three month periods.

❖

Get more readers, more fans and get paid too!

❖

Payout Percentage and Prices

Print version

In your print book on Amazon you will get 60% split of the revenues on your book in the US and most countries (some countries differ and you get less). You get to set your price, but it will show you the minimum price you are allowed to charge. This is because Amazon deducts the printing costs and Amazon still want to make a minimum amount, so it has to cover Amazon's percentage and the printing. You could reduce the book price so you receive nothing or very little, but you can't go lower than Amazon's minimum. You have an incentive to price your book low so that more people will buy it. You will not make as much money on your book sale if you do this, but then your incentive is to make book sales and get your book read, and not care as much about the profits from the actual books. So, in most cases you will want to price your book low.

However, if this doesn't suit you, you can weigh up other options too. Look at what others are charging for a similar book. Alternatively, you may decide another tactic, to keep the price high to give the perception that you and your book are much more valuable.

Usually a price ending in .95 works well. Check out other prices of books in your genre. These prices may be appropriate for your book: $7.95, $9.95, $12.95, $14.95 but Amazon may let you go as low as say $5.45 and then you could price your book at $6.95, be competitive and still make a little money.

Occasionally, Amazon may do a sale on the price of your print book. This is great if they do. You have no control over this, this is something Amazon decides, and you still get your share of the profits. If they do this, there will be a red notation of the new price on Amazon. Unfortunately you can't request this, and they don't give you any notice, so you don't have the notice to do an ad campaign. You just have to check and if Amazon happens to put it on sale, hurry and get an email out as soon as you can.

Kindle Version

For your Kindle version, it will show you a choice option of 35% or 70% payment.

If you do a $0.99 kindle book, you have to go with the 35% option.

If you are going to go with a $2.99 price or higher price, you can have 70% (there is no advantage to checking the 35% box so check the 70% box when you are allowed).

Pricing a book at only $0.99 is going to attract a lot more buyers but because you only get 35%, of the sale, this is very little money. If you price your book at $2.99 believe it or not, this will not attract as many buyers as at $0.99. It really makes that much difference. But in the $2.99 scenario you will make a little money.

If you put your book at $2.98, this will still take you into the 35% bracket, so you only want to go there if you are doing the $0.99 option.

Pricing your e-book at just a little less than print, say $7.95 or $9.95 could also be more appropriate for you, but you will receive much less sales.

What is your incentive here? Is it to get more books out to more people? If so, I recommend $0.99 at 35%. You can change these prices later, so you can test the market.

- $0.99 at 35% – Lots of book sales, lots of readers, not much money

- $2.99 at 70% – Ok book sales, ok readers, you make a little money

- $9.95 at 70% – a lot less book sales, you make much more per book

Other Uploading Notes

The rest of the uploading form is pretty self-explanatory.

- Choose exclusive rights with Amazon if you plan to do the kindle unlimited.

- For copyright, if you wrote it, say yes you own it, even if you have not filed for copyright registration.

- Have your description already written and saved ready to upload. Make sure it is filled with those key words you found.

- You will be asked for your 2 category choices.

- You will be asked for your 7 key word choices.

- You will be asked for your price choices and percentage.

After you upload it, there will be some processing time. For the print version you can order a preview copy which of course will take several days, and there is a delay up to 72 hours for your kindle version to become live.

DAY 30

Marketing

Great, you have now uploaded your book so the sales should start coming in right? Wrong! No one will ever find your book just because you uploaded it. You have to be the driving force, the marketing. Ok, you're right, you are not going to be able to do everything in one day. Marketing is going to be an on-going endeavor. However, you will be able to set up your plan of attack and create your marketing accounts, to set all this into motion.

Marketing

Becoming a Best Seller

Now that your book is live it will show in the description of your book on Amazon that your book appears in certain categories. This is below the information where it shows the number of pages, size etc. This will not show up until you make at least one sale. Then it will show you the ranking of your book, overall and in each of the two categories you chose. The smaller the number, the higher the ranking.

For example, your book may be ranked:

- Amazon Kindle 203,455
- Pets and pet care 3,444
- Exotic animals 2,556

In this example, on the general kindle list of best sellers, your book is ranked over 200,000[th] or there are over 200,000 books ranked higher than yours. In the category "Pets and pet care." you are ranked much higher, at 3444th and in "Exotic animals" slightly better.

Print will have different figures, but they are going to be approximately the same.

In other words, you are way down the list of anyone just finding your book, even in your categories.

Right off the bat, there is an initial period where your book is ranked along side of the New Releases, so at least, at first, your book will be ranked much higher. Then after a short period you will be ranked in with the masses.

This ranking is what you are going to try to increase.

Making your Print Book a Best Seller

Ok, so here is the slightly secret way to make your book an official Amazon "Best Seller." Remember before you uploaded your book, you spent a lot of time deciding on the two categories that are the easiest for your book to get the best ranking. You were looking for the categories that suit your book but that there is not as much competition in. You may have used the program publisherrocket.com to be really accurate about this. So here is what you do. You need to increase your print sales all on one specific day. You are hoping to sell enough books on that day to get you to the top of your category on that day and be ready to screen capture a photo of your book when it does. You may not be able to get your book to stay number one in a category for weeks but hopefully you can get it there for one day, and that's all you need to grab your screen capture.

So now you want to tell everyone you know and call all your friends and tell them to buy your book on that specific day. If you have an email list you want to ask them to buy your new book on that specific day. Note you are not allowed by Amazon rules to compensate anyone for buying your book (or giving you a good review), so you cannot ask them to buy your book and reimburse them or give them an item in return. And it won't count if you just buy a bunch of your own books on that day. The sales have to show different account buyers. So, you have to play fair, and do as much word of mouth, emailing and other advertising as you can, concentrating on the specific day you set.

You can do Amazon paid ads for that day or ads on other book promotion sites such as bookbub.com. You can also do a free kindle book promotion at the same time to bring more general attention to your book and hopefully some print sales (more on this later). You can also set your print price at the lowest price Amazon will allow and change it later. Be careful with this one though as there may be a time delay, so make sure you adjust the price in advance. You cannot choose to put your print book on sale, but you can adjust the print price to the minimum.

❖

Whenever you get to #1 in any category, make sure you photograph it.

❖

How many books do you need to sell to become number one in your category? That depends on the category. It could be as few as 6 or 7 books if your category doesn't have that much competition, but some categories you would need to sell 50 books in that day to rise your book to the top.

As soon as you book reaches number 1 in either of your two categories, click on that category and take a photo. Your book is now an Amazon Best Seller!

New York Times Best Seller
Now this is very different. To be on this list requires the sales of around 10,000 books in a week. And these books can't be all bought from the same source, so you can't just buy them yourself. And people have been known to purchase large amounts of their books. However, if it makes the list there will be a notation next to it that

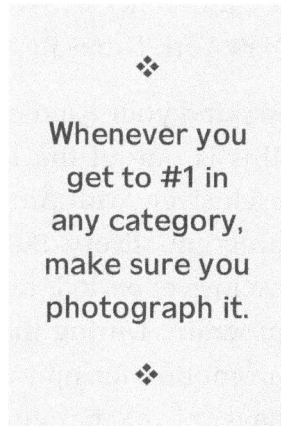

there was a large amount from one source. The notation of Best Seller is very powerful. And a New York Times Best Seller is incredible clout in the publishing industry but honestly most of the general public doesn't know the difference between "best seller" (on Amazon) and a New York Times Best Seller.

Making your Kindle Book a Best Seller

This is one of the reasons you signed your book up exclusively with Amazon and in the Kindle Unlimited program. Every 90 day period, there starts a new exclusive period that your book is enrolled in the program. During that period, you can do a free book promotion for up to five days. That is five consecutive days or five separate days. So here is what I recommend; Choose five consecutive days, commencing at least seven days in advance. Set these dates in the Kindle free book promotion. On those days, your kindle book will be listed as $0 on the "buy now" button. It will also say that your book is free to kindle unlimited subscribers (which it always is when you are in this program), so you need to make it clear to your clients they don't need to subscribe, they can do the "buy now" button for free.

Now the aim here is to advertise a bunch and try to get as many people to download your book for free on those days.

Now you would think that since Amazon lists your book for free, on those days you would get a ton of downloads from Amazon browsers. Absolutely not the case. Unless you tell people, no one notices. You would be amazed at the level of competition of people trying to give away your books for free. There are many websites dedicated to listing the free books on Amazon each day. So, you would also think they would be happy just to list your book for free. Not at all. Yes they do have free listings and you can submit your book but there are many authors vying for the top slot on these free listing websites and so they may charge a premium to be promoted and not just listed. And there are so many of these book promotion sites, and it is so time consuming to list your book with each site there is even a service that will list your free book on these free book listing sites. Here is a link to the service:

**https://bookmarketingtools.com/aff/go/
gailthackray**

I do get a little commission if you use this link, but I do love this service as it saves a ton of time. This service submits your book on the free listing sites for $29. This puts your book on about 20 sites that offer free listings.

The reason I say set your five free days in advance, is because many of these sites require seven days' notice. Some of these sites require all five days consecutive which is a good idea anyway, because as your book hits the Amazon rankings pages it will appear to more customers and it will have a snowball effect.

Some of the free listing sites require a minimum of 5 reviews and a minimum 4.5 stars on these reviews. So, you may need a few reviews first (more on this later).

Then you might want to consider paid advertising on some of these free book listing sites. Bookbub.com is a great one but to get listed on there is highly competitive. You are going to pay between $200 and $300 for a listing and that is only if they accept your book and it is hard to get in. They do accept, pay per impression or per click advertising, without as much difficulty (I recommend per click because at least you know they clicked on the link to your book on Amazon). Yes, I know it seems crazy that you are paying to get people to get your book for free, but the promotion is going to be worth it.

Now besides advertising, you're also going to run posts and ads on social media and through your email list. All your marketing should be concentrating on these five days that your book is going to be free and as much as possible on that first day.

If you do a good ad campaign, you should get 2-3000 downloads of your book and you can see the number of downloads in your kdp portal under reports. This number of downloads is probably good enough to get you to number one in your categories at least some of the time, over your five days. But this is only in the Free Kindle Books and only in your categories. There are listings in Amazon Free Books, both general Amazon

Kindle Free, and for your categories free. Even to get on the first page of the general free Kindle books is hard. I've had 10,000 downloads in a day, on my books and been number one in the free books in my category, but only made it close to the top on the general free books. And this is in the free kindle listings! So, your aim is to try to become number one in your category for free books and as soon as it hits number one, screen capture it!

To get to number one in the regular kindle category (not free), you would employ the same tactics as for print. You would reduce your paid kindle amount to the lowest possible ($0.99) and advertise a ton. Some of the free book listing sites I just mentioned, also list reduced price kindle books at $0.99 as well.

You can also run paid advertising on Amazon per impression or per click (I recommend click). If you are promoting your print book but people see your kindle book is currently free, it's a

❖

TIP–After you have your kindle book free for 5 days, when it goes back to paid, set the price to $0.99. If the reader is just a little late, misses the date and arrives on day six from your promotions, if your book is only $0.99 they may still get it.

❖

no-brainer. However per click costs can be expensive and it can cost you $1 to give away your free kindle book! Per impression is risky as you may get no clicks but when you have a free book promotion running, it might be worth trying an ad running per impression.

❖

TIP–Ok this takes a bit of messing around, but if your kindle book is originally a much higher price, say $9.99 and it goes free, readers often think they are getting a better deal than if it was only $0.99 to start with. So, adjusting your price to a high price before the free period, then free for five days, then a low $0.99 price on day six for a few days, is a good strategy.

❖

Reader Emails

Unfortunately, you do not get customers' emails when they buy your book. You don't get any information at all on the customer. And when you run these ads and your book gets downloaded 10,000 times, you unfortunately don't get any emails or anything. So how do you contact customers? You can't! This is why you put links, your website and your contact information in your book and hope the customer contacts you. You can also put bonus information on your site to encourage the reader to visit your website. Another thing you can do is, when you promote your free book days on social media, instead of sending them direct to Amazon, you can send them to a landing page on your site where you give them more information and then ask them for their email before giving them the Amazon link to your free book.

Paid Amazon Ads

You can promote your book on Amazon buying either impressions or clicks to your book (clicks are more of a safe bet). This works like an auction site, where you can set your highest bid to get someone to click on your book. Amazon reports where the clicks came from, how many sales were made as a result, and the exact income as well as much more detail. You can choose categories, or you can choose other books that are like yours. For the competent advertiser there are many tweaks that you can do.

There is one very interesting metric that Amazon displays as a percentage. That is a percentage of the amount of money spent compared to the amount of money received in your book sales. Here you are trying to get this number under 100, preferable under 70. Basically, if you have opted for the 70% Kindle payout then the amount of money you could afford to spend on advertising would be 70% of the sales. If this metric was 70 then in this case the money you spent on advertising to sell that book, would equal the money you made off that book. This would be your break-even point and you would come out with nothing. (And no money is ok, because you are still getting to readers). But that's not entirely true. You see when you advertise and you are hoping that people will buy your book, they may see your ad but they may be Kindle Unlimited subscribers and they may opt to read your book for free instead. You get paid per page that they read. So even if you make no money on the print sales through your ads, you are still seeing an increase in your monthly revenues through the readers program. So, you could actually let your ad budget go to 100% of your sales and still be ok. If you hit the sweet spot where your ads are making more money than they cost, then it's a no brainer, spend as much as you can, as these ads are profitable. Be very careful though, with paid ads. It is very easy for this metric to go above the 100%, meaning you are spending more than you are bringing back. You need to check constantly, as it is very easy to forget you have an unsuccessful ad running that can run up a huge bill.

Amazon ads can also be set to exact days, so this can be useful when you need that concentrated advertising on one specific day to make your book a best seller. But note, you may set a budget to spend, but Amazon often does not reach that maximum budget because others are out-bidding you. If you set your ad budget to spend $100 a day but your bid is low, Amazon may only spend $10 a day and you may not have the traffic you wanted on that day, so your bid will have to be competitive to spend the budget you want to spend.

Kindle Unlimited

We have touched on this already. When your book is enrolled in this program, readers who are subscribers can read your book for free. There is an Amazon pool of funds each month and this is divided between all the books in the program, based on the number of pages read. It only counts one read per person, so if a person reads your book multiple times that doesn't count. The total amount will often be a significant amount compared to your print sales. For example, if your print sales for a month are $1800, your kindle unlimited payment might be around $1200. I am going off my experience here, so this may not be the same for everyone and may differ for different types of book. But, I believe this is definitely worth doing. And remember you care about the exposure and how many people read your book and not so much on the revenues off the actual book. Authors who plan to make more per kindle sale and set a higher price for their kindle book would likely not enroll in this program as you are going to lose kindle sales to people who have Unlimited Kindle accounts. But we care more about promotion of you and your brand and getting your book read more often.

Reviews

I can't tell you how important reviews are. Particularly 5 star reviews. There is no easy way to get reviews. Apparently, in the past there were freelancers that would write reviews for a fee, but Amazon clamped down on them. You also have to be careful never to offer to compensate people, by either directly paying them, or even by giving them an item or putting them in a sweepstakes or something. This is against Amazon rules and could get you banned. So, you can ask people nicely for a review and hope for the best. You can give away copies of your book and say you would appreciate an honest review. You can't even ask for a good review, you can only ask for an honest opinion! There are some services that are legitimate that will put you in contact with readers who would like to receive your book for free and have offered to write a review, but there is no guarantee they will. These have some success, but they are not cheap. You can also go to people on Amazon who have reviewed books similar to yours, and if they have a public profile, offer them your book for free saying you'd appreciate a review. Bottom line is, you have to keep asking your followers nicely.

There are companies that will write a book summary for you. This is different. These are companies that will read your book and write a summary that you can use in your description, but they will NOT give you a rating or review from their account. Similarly, if your friends or fans email you a "review," you can use this on your site, but it doesn't help you with reviews on Amazon. You need the person to log in from their account and submit the review to Amazon.

Then on the rating, you need those 5 star ratings. Sometimes people give a good review and a 4 star rating. I don't think people understand that a 4 star rating is not good, and is going to really hurt you. On Airbnb and Uber a 4 star average gets you thrown off the platform. An Amazon 5 star rating that just says two words such as "good book," is far more valuable to you than a two paragraph glowing review and 4 stars. And then there will be those that give you a 1 or 2 star rating. Usually they haven't even read your book but have found you through other means and just don't like you. You will find that as you become more successful there will be haters. This is an unpleasant side of being a public figure. As you launch your successful speaking career, you are going to come across jealous people and they will find your book and rate you down. These people are never successful themselves, and hate seeing others succeed. There is not much you can do about these, life is too short.

Become an Amazon Affiliate

You can sign up to become an Amazon Affiliate. This is a separate program where you can promote Amazon products and receive a small percentage of what the customer spends. You are even allowed, as an author to present your book through an affiliate link. Meaning, you are already advertising your book, if you are an Amazon Affiliate you can use an affiliate link to advertise your book. So not only do you benefit from the sale of your book as the author, you can also get a small fee as the marketer of your book. It is not much, (usually 10% depending on the product), but it is something. And if after looking at your book they decide to buy something else on Amazon, you also get a percentage of those sales (if they qualify). It is important to note that you have to make the customer aware that you receive a portion of the sale, using the Amazon wording on your sales page.

You can also combine your book with other offers. Let's say you have a health and fitness book. You can create a page that has your book and also offers other products from Amazon such as an exercise device and a health drink, you choose off Amazon. You now receive a small commission from any of these sales you drive to Amazon.

Print on Demand – Order Print Copies of your book

These days, Amazon does not stock large amounts of books in warehouses. Rather when the customer orders your book, it is only then printed and shipped to the customer. This is called, "Print on Demand." For this reason, your book should always display as "in stock." If it goes out of stock, and you are publishing through kindle direct publishing, contact them, as there is an error.

You are also going to want to order print copies of your book to sell at your speaking events, workshops, and other avenues you may have. It is quite easy to order copies through the kindle kdp portal. The price is based on the size of the book and number of pages and the number of units you order, but to give you an idea the average book is going to cost you $3.50 to $5 per book, plus shipping. These orders are not the same as a customer ordering one of your books on Amazon, these print runs take much longer, about 3-4 weeks. Make sure you allow the time, especially if you need them for an event. You can also put any shipping address in, so you can also have them shipped directly to an event.

Other Printers and Publishers

It used to be that there were several alternatives to uploading your book to Amazon directly and there were several options to load your book onto Amazon. Amazon has made it so easy to load your book directly there is not much incentive to work with others. I have used Lightningsource.com as both a distributor and printer, and still do some work through them, if you want to check them out as an alternative. They have printing presses in New York, Sydney and London. If you are doing large batches of printing it is worth checking out different printing and shipping options. Also, I discovered that it is much cheaper if I am travelling to an event to have the printer ship the books directly to the location. Having books delivered first to you and then on to the location is much more expensive. Books are heavy, it is worth extra planning to decide how many books you will need and making arrangements for moving left-overs back to you after the event.

Book Store Distributors and Wholesalers

If you can get your book into a major bookstore this would bring tremendous exposure and credibility to your brand. However, getting your book into bookstores is not easy. If you opted for the extended distribution through Amazon, you may get some book placement in stores, but I wouldn't hold your breath. These large chains are still looking for the top sellers and big-name authors. Large chain bookstores deal with distributors, large publishers and of course Amazon, but not individual authors and even then, they rarely stock books from relatively unknown authors. Getting into bookstores is where the top publishing names have a lot of clout. Going to a Barnes and Noble, as one unknown author would be near impossible. Publishers are spending a tremendous amount of marketing money to get to these bookstores and to get the best display of the newest hot sellers that they have. There is little chance of independent publishers getting their one title in a large chain bookstore, without going through a wholesaler, distributor, or larger publisher.

As an author you would have a better shot visiting small mom and pop bookstores. They may be happy for you to do an in-person book signing at their store.

Look for bookstores that are specific to your genre. Sometimes, just the fact that you are a local author to them, might be enough to promote you. Even the small specialty bookstores, usually buy their books through wholesalers who have catalogs of many books to choose from. It is simply too much tracking and accounting for book shops to deal with individual authors and they only usually make exceptions if you are doing a live appearance in their store. Once you start speaking in different cities, you will find it extremely beneficial if you can do some book signing appearances in some local bookshops while you are there.

There are middlemen distributors or wholesalers who are the go between from the publishers to the stores. In the "New-Age" genre where I have written many books, a great wholesaler who I work with is called New Leaf Distributing Company (**https://newleafvendors. com**). They have hundreds of books from hundreds of authors all in the meta-physical genre. They produce a catalog that goes out to specialty shops interested in these types of books. The bookstore gets your book at a discount, usually paying 50-55% of the retail price. The wholesaler then takes a small percentage, so you get about 40%. Out of this money you are responsible for the printing costs and shipping the books to the wholesaler's warehouse. This is a great way to get your books into smaller book shops. As always, to get the best out of this, you are going to want to purchase display ads in their catalog and on their catalog site and their emails to bookstores. At the end of the day, after you pay for the shipping, you are not making much money per book. But again, what is your real incentive here? You are looking to gain more customers who will read your book as well as that brand awareness and credibility to customers browsing the bookstores.

You can ask the bookshops that you want to get into, where they order their books from and then approach those wholesalers.

If you do get picked up with a distributor, then it is a great idea to contact bookstores that regularly purchase from their catalog and ask about doing an appearance in their store. That way they know when they have you as a guest in their shop, they already are able to buy your book on-going through their regular catalog.

Audio Book

You have already written your book, why not create an audio book? This is additional wonderful promotion for your brand without too much effort. You can record this in portions, perhaps one or two chapters at a time. It is going to take you a little time, but it's worth it. If your book reads a total of eight hours as a final product, you are probably going to spend at least double that time in recording it.

Audible is a great program and it is connected to Amazon. Create an account with Audible and start by entering your book which it will link from Amazon. You actually have to have it published on Amazon first.

Choose whether you want to be exclusive with Audible and receive a higher payout, or be non-exclusive for a lower payout, if you are planning on putting your book on other audio platforms. I recommend going exclusive, unless you have plans to do something else specifically with the audio.

Now you have a choice of recording this yourself or partnering with a voice over artist on Audible. If you record it yourself, of course you will keep a larger share of the profits. I would say, if you are comfortable recording it yourself, this is the better way to go. Remember, you are promoting your brand, so your voice and your personality is going to be the best way to present your book. Again, your goal here is to brand you, as a speaker, as a coach, as a public figure or the representative for your company or product.

If you really have too difficult of a time doing this, you can partner with a voice over artist through audible and you will find instructions on the Audible site. In this case Audible pays the artist their percentage directly.

If you are going to record this yourself, you can either go to a professional studio to be recorded or you can do it fairly adequately at home. Personally, I record them myself, on my computer. If you are going to be recording this in about 20 different sessions, each one or two hours, it is much more convenient to do at home. For this, you will need a decent mic. Your computer built in mic is probably not good enough quality. I recommend the Blue Yeti mic, which you can find on Amazon. Add a mic foam cover or sound bounce shield. Then find a place that is going to block out most of the environmental sound. The best scenario is if you could make a makeshift sound studio in a room or your garage, with some foam insulation on the walls. If you can't do this, find as quiet a room as possible. You will do some recording tests to find out the best mic placement to get the best sound.

Then you will need some editing software. I use a simple free software called Audacity which you can download free here: **https://www.audacityteam.org/** This records your files which you can save in MP3 or Wave format. There will be a little bit of sound clean up needed. You do not want any extreme swings in the volume, so no harsh peaks. You can record each chapter individually, in any order, and you need to leave a few seconds before and after each chapter. There are very specific tech specs you need to follow on Audible. I am not experienced enough to edit the recordings, so I record each chapter and send to a sound editor who cleans up any peaks and errors and my screw ups. Most of this you can probably do yourself in Audacity.

You will upload each cleaned up track as chapters into Audible. There is a delay of at least 10 days while they review it and they may have changes. Then there is additional processing time.

Once it is live, you can promote your audible book using the affiliate links that they give you. Through your affiliate link, if a person listens to your book or joins audible through you, you receive an additional commission on top of your book royalties.

Also, when you are promoting your book on Amazon, you are also automatically promoting your audio book as well, since they are linked, so your marketing efforts to your kindle and print book will automatically advertise your audio version. In many cases people will get your book and then the audio version as well.

❖

TIP – There are going to be screw ups and you cannot keep going back to the beginning to get a clean take. So, when I screw up and blunder a word, I do a loud shout or bell or foghorn. And then just repeat and keep going. This way when you look at the track later, you can visually see a large jump in volume and go right to that point to fix the audio.

❖

It is also great to promote your affiliate audible links directly on your social media and to your email subscribers.

Unfortunately, there are no free giveaway audible promotions, other than a few links Audible provides you to start with. Don't just give these to your best friends. These links are best used to give to people or sites that will review your audio book or your top customers.

If you are non-exclusive with Audible, you can promote your audio book through chirpbooks.com, a subsidiary of bookbubs.com (where you did the free kindle promotions) but you will need to upload your audio book to the Findaway platform.

Making Your Book into an Online Course

You already have a book why not consider recording a video of your subject matter for an online course? If you wrote an "how to" book, then record a "how to," video course. You can bundle your video clips with your ebook pdf or turn your book into separate worksheets. Check out the platforms Teachable.com and Udemy.com where you can upload your online course. Think about other content that you could add to your course such as interviewing others on your subject. You can even offer an in person, or online course for a select group of clients and as long as you have their permission, use this footage to add into your course.

Selling Your Books at Events

Now you are a published "best-selling" author, you can use this to launch your speaking or coaching career. At your events you want to get out as many books as you can. These people are your prime audience that you could potentially turn into on-going customers. Your book is your calling card that you want every customer to get. You should of course be promoting and selling your books at your events. Since you are not tied to a publisher and forced to sell your book for a certain price, you can also do some create marketing at these events to get your book to as many interested customers as possible. Perhaps you reduce the price to your actual printing costs to encourage your customers to get a copy. Perhaps you create a package of a free book with every paid workshop attendee. Perhaps you give a free book with a product purchase or you could do a raffle or drawing for a free book. A raffle for a free book is a great way to talk about your book and a great way to collect emails. And just the fact that you are there personally signing your books will be a great incentive for your customers to purchase a copy. Remember your biggest incentive is to get your book to customers and get them to read it and secondary is the money you might make from selling the book itself.

Funnels and Upsells

Funnels is a concept that has been used in business long before it was given the name of "funnel" and it is a very effective way to build your audience.

If people do not know you, they are not going to read your book, buy anything from you, and especially not make a large purchase from you. It is very important that you share enough of yourself with your potential customer that they can understand what you are all about, what your product or service is, and more than anything, trust you.

And why would you? I know, for me personally I am willing to pay for something, but I first want to have some kind of sample, to find out if I am interested, and if they can really deliver what they say. There is so much choice for consumers in every area, especially to attend workshops, and so it is important that you show people first what you can do.

I am a big proponent of giving away free stuff. Meaning, inviting people to get to know you with no charge at all, or very little charge, and giving your time and possibly tangible goods for free. In fact, I believe in over delivering amazing content for free. And then once a customer has gotten to know you, you can offer an extra service item or service for a small charge and then from there offer a much larger ticket item for the select few of those that are interested and willing to commit to a larger service.

And that is the premise of the funnel; start out with a free service or very low cost service, then some of those people will be interested in an additional higher cost service, then out of those people a few will be interested in a significantly higher purchase or exclusive service.

For instance, this could be a free one hour seminar filled with tons of content where the attendees are given the opportunity to attend another perhaps all day workshop for $100-200 and for those who are really committed an offer of a trip or an item that would be several thousand dollars.

If 1000 people attended your free workshop, about 200 of those people would sign up for your paid day workshop as well as buy a book from you. Out of the 200 that buy your paid workshop, about 40 of them would buy a higher ticket item or attend a higher priced exclusive event. And many of these people become customers who continue to support you for years. In my experience, if you just tried to market your higher priced event to get those 40 people you would have a much harder time. And there are people from the rest of the initial 1000 that will over time buy some items, attend events, and spread the word to their friends.

I have found from experience that in the long run, the initial free lecture is many times more valuable to me. This is because, I collect customers and their emails. Most people who attend a free seminar and feel they received a lot of useful content, are likely to want to buy a book or item almost as a "thank you," and these people go on to buy many products, workshops and events.

A book itself is a form of a funnel. You are using the book as the tool where your customer can get to know you, to hear your story. Then you can over deliver on great content in your book and get them begging for more.

A new concept that has sprung up online is that of a "free book, you just pay shipping." Many people are doing this, and often they use a template service called Clickfunnels. com. You may have seen these ads on Facebook and Instagram. This is where an author is giving you their book for the shipping only, usually $7.95 or $9.95 US and $14.95 or $19.95 international. In reality, this amount will probably cover the cost of printing as well as the postage (if you do media mail which takes a little longer but is specifically for books). So, you are giving away your book for free. It's not costing you anything, but you are probably not making anything either. But you are actually gaining a customer that is reading your book and getting to know and love you (exactly your purpose). And you are also gaining their email to build your future customer list. Also, on this same free book form, especially if you set it up through Clickfunnels.com, you probably see an upsell item. This could be, "get the free book but also get my online webinar/coaching/other item for an additional $xx." You already have their credit card for the shipping of the free book, so it is easier to get them to check an extra box, and they don't need to enter their credit card again. And possibly you'll see an additional upsell, such as, "get my personal one-on-one coaching/ my Holy Grail item for $xxxxx," (again, just a check box because you already have their credit card), followed by a possible down-sell, such as, ok you didn't go for the Holy Grail so how about a lesser price for ...

I do think the "free book just pay shipping" works great. Clickfunnels.com is a great way to do it. I believe Clickfunnels.com charges $295 per month after a free trial, to use their many templates, billing features, ad templates and other features. If you are just offering your book free and don't have your upsell yet, you could also just send the user to your store or landing page, to collect the "shipping."

On a larger scale you are going to do Facebook and Instagram marketing of your free book promotion. You will have to test your images, copy and graphics to figure out what is your best return. It is going to cost you for this advertising, and you are not making much profit, if anything, on the money, as it is going to your printing and mailing costs. However, you are getting your book to many more customers and building your customer lists, which is extremely valuable. Facebook and Instagram marketing is not cheap, so you will probably have to have some higher ticket upsells to really make it work and make a profit here.

This free book, just pay shipping, of course works on mailing physical print books to a person. You can't say free book and pay for shipping on your e-book, because obviously the customer knows there is no shipping costs. You can be creative though and say; I'll send you an item (small product related to your book) for free, just pay shipping, and I'll email you my ebook as a bonus. You can say, free ebook, and just ask for their email.

Be creative, think of ways you can bundle products that you have; your print book, ebook, audio book (you will not be able to give an Audible book link, you would have to send the audio files if you are non-exclusive), bundled with webinars, online courses, coaching sessions and physical items related to your book. On the physical items related, they are going to have to be something you have, can stock, or have dropped shipped as you will not be able to send them through your Amazon affiliate code.

Market Testing

In all your marketing start small. Test all the different methods and all social media to find out what works for you. Test by changing one thing, such as changing out just a photo or just a line of copy. Do small dollar runs, until you get the right combination of photo, text and audience. When you are certain your ad is profitable, now you can't lose.

TIME TO FLY

Now you are a published best-selling author! Now your speaking and coaching business can really fly! Make sure you continue to interact with your audience and value your customers. When you continue to provide your customers with fresh, new, interesting content they will support you and guide you.

For bonus material, and a list of all the sites, vendors and useful links go here:

GailThackray.com/write-my-book

ABOUT THE AUTHOR

Gail Thackray is an author, speaker and success coach who believes we can be both materially successful and lead a spiritually empowered life.

She is the author of 15 "best sellers." Including, *"30 Days to Prosperity: A Workbook to Manifest Abundance," "What's Up with Your Life? Finding and Living Your True Purpose,"* and several spiritual books on Natural Healing, Reiki and Developing Intuition.

Gail has a background as an entrepreneur running her own photo stock library business that at the height of the Internet was valued at $50 million dollars. Gail more recently wrote an entertainment expose book about this time, *"Running with Wolves: a Woman's Memoir of Sex Scandal and Seduction."*

Gail has a podcast *"Finding Your Sexiness,"* encouraging people to find their purpose and passion in business and in life. Gail helps people to find their true calling and become leaders, speakers and coaches in their chosen field.

Gail was raised in Yorkshire, England and is now based in Los Angeles.

To find out more about Gail, her other books, her TV series and workshops, or to find out how you can visit her at a live event near you, please visit her website: **www.GailThackray.com**